HEAVEN

If You Want In

REGISTER NOW!

Michael W. Dewar

DWELLING PLACE
Publishers

ISBN: 979-8-9856973-7-7 (Paperback)
ISBN:979-8-9856973-6-0 (eBook)

Dwelling Place Publishers
PO Box 360193 · Brooklyn, NY 11236
DPSCleamsing.com

Unless otherwise indicated, Bible quotations are taken from The Holy Bible, New International Version(NIV). Copyright © 1973, 1978, 1984 by International Bible Society; The Holy Bible, King James Version(KJV), or the New King James Version (NKJV); or, The Holy Bible, English Standard Version (ESV). All Copyright material used by permission.

Dedication

This book is dedicated to all my family members, friends, and acquaintances who are not yet registered to the Lamb's book of life in heaven. My prayer is that your relationship with Jesus Christ will be established soon, for then and only then you can be certain that you are truly registered in heaven.

CONTENTS

PREFACE

This is not your usual book about heaven. The author did not have a near death experience in which his dying brain saw a bright light causing him to conclude he was in heaven or on his way to heaven. The author does not take a position on those fancy, Hollywood-like stories, whether they are true or false.

Furthermore, this book does not debate the question whether heaven or hell exists or not. Such issues have been debated enough over many centuries, and a generous number of books written and available in the marketplace on them.

This author takes the position that you either believe in heaven and hell or you do not. If you have compelling evidence for whatever conclusion you reached on these subjects, present them. My mission is not to convert you from one to the other.

Even if the Word of God did not tell us there is a heaven to gain and a hell to avoid, basic common sense tells us there must be such places. Any kingdom or nation State that has respect for justice and human decency must have a judicial system, including law enforcement and a prison system.

Well, there is the Kingdom of God and God Himself who is the primary lawgiver. If He is going to enforce His own laws, He must have created a judicial system to protect the innocent and punish the guilty. What is so difficult about that for reasonable people to agree on? That is one reason this book does not devote space to discuss whether hell or heaven exist or not. It is basic common-sense that a righteous God would have a system of justice in place. That is what the judgment of God, heaven, and hell are all about, and the Bible speaks decisively about them.

This book is written as a supplement to my 10-volume series, *Related Events to the Second Coming of the Christ*. Each volume in the series deals with at least one major event in the unfolding drama of the end-time happening before our eyes. Since, no sane person wants to go anywhere other than heaven, this book is written to help you get there. It is also written to supplement another work titled, *The Book of Life & The Books of Wrath*.

If you have other eternal destinations in mind because you neither believe in heaven or hell—chance are, you may not benefit from this book. Nonetheless, I am still inviting you to give it a good read. You never know what pleasant surprises the blessed Holy Spirit has in store.

Thanks to all of you for your support of this ministry, by buying these books, giving them to friends and families, and writing customers' reviews on Amazon and other places, you partner with me in the work of God, such partnership pays eternal dividends. Thanks!

INTRODUCTION

This book deals with serious issues of life that most of us would rather put off for a more convenient day, a day that will never come for most people. You will be tempted to browse quickly through this work, then put it aside thinking when you have the time, you will give it a good read. But in most cases, we never get back to it, so resist the temptation. There are urgent matters we need to confront with courage, and we need to do so now because waiting for tomorrow is too risky.

I have always wondered why the things that are important and necessary provide so little fun or sense of urgency. For example, as children we had to be prodded to eat our vegetables and take our medicine. As adults, we tend to have the same attitude about buying life insurance and preparing a will; we always want to put off doing them for a more convenient day. Why? On second thought, I know why. These things make us uncomfortable. Life insurance and drafting a will remind us of our mortality, something we would rather not think about.

Reading this book will give you that same sense discomfort, but it is important. So, let us embrace the discomfort and get on with the reading. The benefits are good for time and eternity. Let us begin with a fun story, not so funny when you think about it.

My mother was a good story-teller. When I was a little boy, she told me and one of my sisters this story about Tom Wilmore (not his real name) who was a bad man, evil. Nobody liked him.

Yet, he was married to this wonderful Christian woman who would do anything to turn Tom's life around. But the more she prayed for him the worse he got. That was the way it appeared to her, and it made her very unhappy, but she kept praying for a turnaround in Tom's life, nonetheless.

Tom fell asleep on the couch washing the TV one night and had a dream. He dreamed that the devil was having a conference with his top executives, and he, Tom, was the topic under discussion. The devil said, "We are expecting Tom Wilmore down here, but we do not have space for him. Wilmore is a troublemaker; he will be a big problem for us." One demon suggested giving Wilmore matches to start his own hell. The devil said, "Brilliant!"

But about that time Wilmore showed up and was told there is no vacancy; he started an argument and demanded to see the boss. The devil showed up and confirmed there was no vacancy and gave him matches to go start his own hell. But Wilmore told the devil, "I will start my own hell right here!" He started a fight, and the devil kicked him, and he went up in a puff of smoke.

At this point, Wilmore jumped out of his sleep screaming and wet with perspiration as one escaping from a hot oven. His wife calmed him down from his terrifying nightmare. He said,

"It is bad enough to go to hell, but to get kicked out of hell is unbearable." From that night, Wilmore gave his heart to the Lord and later became a deacon in the church.

This is a funny, fictitious story about one man's dream that changed his life and caused him to start a relationship with Jesus Christ, and by it became registered in the Lamb's Book of Life in heaven. There is nothing else fictitious about this book and what we must all face now or hereafter. It will make you uncomfortable but embracing the discomfort now and boldly starting your own relationship with Jesus Christ will get you registered in heaven for time and eternity. Once you are registered, it brings a good feeling to you like none other.

With this book you are starting a journey into a spiritual experience, and I am your guide to get you started. You might have begun this journey years ago. If so, there are certain things that are familiar to you, but now you are going fine-tune that journey and fill in the blanks. I want to walk you into the future, so when that future comes, you know what to expect because you have already been there and positioned yourself for the best it has to offer. I guarantee you, a future in Christ has everything.

Or you can wait, do not take the journey, and be dreadfully surprised at the future that is rapidly moving toward you. To wait is not the wise choice, because you have everything to lose.

If you have not already done so, upon completing this volume, you have a ten-volume series to complete, each one is about the same size of this book. The series is called, *Related Events to the Second Coming of the Christ.* Each volume deals with at least one major event that you will be involved in as a winner or a loser. To be an informed person on the winning side, follow carefully the guidance given in this volume. The ten volumes are listed at the back of this book and available on

Amazon. Since one volume builds upon the other, they should be read one volume at a time beginning with volume one.

There are two additional volumes to read to round out your knowledge of the future that is already here. They are *The Book of Life and the Books of Wrath*, and *A Working Vacation in Heaven*? Now, in the end, nothing in these thirteen volumes will benefit you if you are not Registered in the Lamb's Book of Life in heaven. You must register before physical death comes to you, otherwise all opportunity of registration will be lost. Come with me as I brief you on the chapters in this volume in your hands.

In Chapter 1, we look at your value and worth as a human being. This is not your financial worth but your worth as God sees you. I hope you will see yourself as God sees you. You are His image bearer and a person with potential for heaven.

Chapter 2 goes on to examine the reality of heaven against the biblical text. It is a real place, as real as earth. Chapter 3 does the very opposite. It looks at the eternal prison known as hell, shows you why it was created, and why it is necessary.

Chapter 4 looks at how one gets to heaven. It refutes several misconceptions contrary to what the Word of God teaches. You will find that getting into heaven is much different from what popular opinion wants you to believe.

Chapter 5 guides you through the registration process. There are those who refuse to register; chapter 6 addresses the reality of their eternal destination. The last chapter is seven, it gives a brief sample of the benefits that will come to those who are registered citizens of heaven. This book is intended to be read reflectively, contemplatively, not in a mad rush. Take your time.

CHAPTER 1

WHAT IS YOUR WORTH?

W ho are you? What is your value? Why are you here, and where are you going from here? These are questions of identity, self-worth, purpose, and destination. Research has shown that people who live fulfilled lives are the ones who have confronted these questions and have answered them honestly.

People who ignore these questions are the ones most likely to end up unfulfilled and lost. They lived but did not discover their true self-worth or know why they lived. Miles Munroe said, "The greatest tragedy in all of life is to live and don't know why."[1] This book will help you avert such tragedy.

People who can answer the preceding four questions honestly and satisfactorily to themselves are the ones who have begun to understand the significance of life. They discover that human life goes beyond mere physical existence of breathing, eating, working, satisfying our desires, and dying. Humans are also spiritual beings who are eternal, and we are faced with two eternal choices: eternal life and eternal death (John 3:16-18).

We must always keep eternity in view because that is where we are heading by deliberate choice or by default. The default choice is not good. This truth is foundational in all of Scripture, including the teachings of Jesus (Matthew 6:19-24).

It is for this spiritual and eternal side of human existence why it is most important to secure heaven as your ultimate destination choice. If your answer to the first question ("Who am I?") is vague, you are likely to be vague on the second and third questions as well. If that is the case for you, your eternal destination will not appear meaningful now. You are likely to leave it to chance, but that is a risk that no one should take.

This book is pressing you not to take such foolish risk, but to urgently make a positive destination plan now. Make it your number one and necessary priority. The vast multitudes of humanity are stampeding down a broad way with no inclination that the bridge is down (Matthew 7:13-14). They have ignored every warning! When we are healthy and doing well, this is not the conversation most of us want to have, but life can change in the blink of an eye, leaving us no time to plan.

As a rationale for this book, this chapter explores the four questions asked in the opening paragraph. Then it prods you to reflect on these questions. It is my attempt to slow us down from the hectic pace of life and divert us all from the stampede. It is an attempt to have us refocus on things spiritual, things eternal; the things once gained, we cannot lose.

We are so busy making a name for ourselves, pursuing what some call, the American dream, that we put our souls at risk without realizing it. The dream has illuded many of us as an enchanting mirage in the distance, yet it still beckons us to keep up the illusive chase. This mad pursuit of things has left many shipwrecked on the high seas of life.

Others have achieved their dream, but it has turned out to be a nightmare in the end, leaving them empty and meaningless, rich in things but poor in soul. If you are one of them, you are invited to change your focus to a more certain and promising future. Fix your gaze on our Lord Jesus Christ, He will carry you across the finish line with heavenly applauses (Hebrews 12:1-3).

King Solomon of ancient Israel was a man who chased pleasure and things until he lost sight of the God who made him great; he came up empty and broken in heart. He cautions us with these sobering words, "Remember now your Creator in the days of your youth, before the days of trouble come and the years approach when you will say, I have no pleasure in them" (Ecc. 12:1). When we pursue things without God, we can lose everything in the process, even our souls if we are not careful.

The four questions force us to look at ourselves seriously as we navigate our short earthly life. The questions have eternal implications worth considering because the stakes are too high to ignore. So, let us explore these questions together.

Who are you?

In the first-person singular, "who are you" becomes who am I? It is a question of personal identity, knowing oneself. Socrates in his philosophy used the maxim, "Man know thyself." As a teacher, Socrates knew that a person knows nothing until he knows himself. Self-discovery is the most important discovery of all discoveries. You come to know who you are.

It is fascinating to observe a child in the process of discovering self. In this self-revelation, the child comes to understand that he or she is a separate person from mother. Soon thereafter, the child begins to move away from mother and to say, no! Armed with this one word, a child can exert his will to the frustration of parents or any other adult.

We know ourselves in relationship with others: parents, siblings, guardians, friends, and community members. If you grew up as a feral child, you have no human association; animals of the lower creation socialized you. And you behave as wild and untamed as they do, because you think you are one of them. But the fact is, you are a higher order of being.

The Bible presents Adam and Eve as the first humans. They were created as full-grown adults. They had no feral childhood because they were never children, so they were not socialized by the brute, beast of the lower creation.

Adam was created sometime before his companion Eve. And in that time of aloneness, he never considered the animals his equal. He did not take a companion from among them, because none was suitable for him. He gave names to the animals, thus demonstrating his intelligence and superiority over them (Genesis 2:19-20). Naming and categorizing things is what we call the discipline of taxonomy today. Adam worshiped and fellowshipped with God, the Being of highest superiority.

God said, "It was not good for the man to be alone." Since there was not a suitable companion for Adam among the animals, God took one of Adam's ribs and created woman. Right away Adam recognized her as his equal. He said, now this is bone of my bone and flesh of my flesh, she shall be called woman because she was taken out of man" (Genesis 2:18, 20-25). Adam discovered himself and he discovered Eve as a suitable companion. God married them and blessed them to be fruitful and multiply. A beautiful story indeed!

It is not good for man to be alone; that includes woman. What does that mean? We can now think of a thousand reasons, but when it was first said there were two immediate and apparent reasons: 1) everything else had a mate and a mandate to produce after its kind, except Adam, and 2) Adam had to further distinguish himself from the brute/beast creation and from God. He was not one or the other. He was not on the brute's level, and he was not equal with God, who was he?

Adam discovered who he was when Eve came along. We discover our true selves in relationships. If you want to know who you are—look at your neighbors; they are flawed as you are. But if you want to know who you ought to be—look at Jesus Christ. He is the only perfect, human example available, with whom to have a pleasing, and acceptable relationship with God. That is why the two greatest commandments are love for God, and love for neighbor. Neighbor now includes all your fellow human beings, even your enemies (Matthew 5:43-48).

God does not want us to degenerate to the level of the brute/beast, thus becoming less than what we were created for (Romans 1:18-32). Nor does God want us to usurp His position. That has been the temptation of humans from the Paradise Garden until now, stepping out of our assigned role for something lesser or greater than that for which we were created. The irony and folly is—we cannot be God, and we will not be angels, so in either way we end up being like the devil.

Adam and His wife fell because they failed to obey an executive order issued by their Superior (God). They chose to listen to Satan because he led them to believe they could be wise as God himself (Genesis 3:4-5). The temptation was for them to usurp God's position. They did and the outcome was death and expulsion from Paradise (Genesis 3:22-24). Before that, Satan had usurped his position and got thrown out of heaven (Isaiah 14; Ezekiel 28, Revelation 12).

There is a relationship humans had with God in the Paradise Garden that is not yet fully restored. It is restored in Jesus Christ to a degree, but it is a process that is still unfolding. After the Fall, Adam had fellowship with God, but it was never the same as before the Fall. Before the Fall, Adam and Eve were able to see God face to face. Face to face fellowship will not be restored until the new world order when God relocates, brings the New Jerusalem to suspended over the new earth (Revelation 21:1-5).

At that time, we are no longer banished from the tree of life, Eden is restored, and we can see God face to face again. But notice that this restoration takes place after the Final Judgment when sin, disease, suffering, death and Satan and evil are removed from the creation, and we are living in a completely new creation. This is what you are invited to register for in this book. You must be registered in the Lamb's book of life now to share in the enjoys of the new world order. You are invited to register because you worth it!

What is your value?

You have value and worth above the brute/beast because you were created in the image and likeness of your Creator (Genesis 1:27). Again, it is in relationship with God and neighbor the we discover our true value and worth. No one knows the value and worth of a thing as the maker or creator of that thing.

Our Creator values human life supremely. To God, human life is sacred, and He protects its sanctity by law. When Cain murder his brother, Abel, God held Cain accountable for the shedding of innocent blood, destroying human life (Genesis 4).

After the great flood, God made it clear again to Noah and his generation that human life is sacred. He enacted a law demanding the life of any animal or person who takes the life of a human being (Genesis 9:1-7). Under Moses, God included murder as one of the Ten Commandments (Exodus 20:13).

God is reasonable in this matter of a human being taking the life of another. He distinguished accidental death from a life premeditatedly taken; the former He calls, manslaughter, and the latter murder. Death was not required for manslaughter, but the comfort of life was interrupted for the manslayer, even though he was shown mercy (Numbers 35:6-34).

God has made it clear that all human beings are the image bearer of God, and He placed immense value and worth on each human life. Any human who deliberately takes the life of another or cause that life to be taken has forfeited his own life. God gave human government the power of the sword to enforce this law in the context of due process (Genesis 9:5-6; Romans 13:1-7).

From the creation of the first humans in Genesis (1:26-27), God has demonstrated the value and worth of human life. Redemption which began immediately after the Fall is another demonstration of how God feels about human beings. They are so valuable to Him that He became a man in the person of Jesus Christ to rescue them (John 3:16).

This rescue mission of redemption will continue to unfold until God vanquishes evil from His creation. That includes all opposing forces and personalities: sin, Satan and his angels, sickness, disease, pain, and suffering, even death itself (Revelation 20:11-15). When that is accomplished, God will recreate a new heaven and a new earth for His beloved human family and relocate to dwell with them (Revelation 21).

This is the context in which God views human value and worth, and He wants you to view yourself no less. You are part of something supremely great and awe-inspiring. This book invites you to be proactive in this great drama of God's redemption plan for us humans. You are called upon to be proactive, securing your own place in God's kingdom by registering now. You worth it!

Why are you here?

Why are you here? This is a question of geographical awareness and purpose. Look up at the heavens! Look at the picturesque and majestic scenes that surrounds you and ask, why am I here? "Why" has to do with purpose. "Here" has to do with place. This question demands an answer if life is going to be meaningful.

A meaningful life has awareness of time and place, and it is *purpose driven*. However, if you know who you are (*your identity*) and you know your value and worth (*image bearer of the Divine*), chances are—you already know your purpose, or at least, close to discovering it. But there is a danger of having lived yet not knowing why. That is most tragic!

You do not want to be numbered among them for they are the same people who do not know where they are going from here. Destination is the connection between the now and the future. If you are not aware of the now (the present time), to you the future is not particularly important. Life without geography is meaningless; that is why no one wants to be homeless.

God created humans as part of His family to represent Him in the earth realm (geography). Solomon, the wise King of ancient Israel did the research for us. He studied all of life, searching to discover where humans could find meaning during their short lifespan on this earth. He gives us the following intelligence report:

> Now all has been said; here is the conclusion of the matter; Fear God and keep his commandments, for this is the duty of all mankind. For God will bring every deed into judgment, including every hidden thing, whether it is good or evil (Ecclesiastes 12:13-14 NIV).

In the preceding quotation, Solomon wraps the duty and purpose of humankind in the same paper. Our duty or purpose here is to fear or serve God and keep His commandments. When you read the commandments, you will see that our duty or purpose here is to serve both God and neighbor (Exodus 20:1-17; Mark 12:28-30). The Westminster Catechism asserts that "Man's chief purpose is to enjoy God and serve Him forever."

Solomon further asserts that God will bring us into judgment with everything we do here on earth, whether it be good or evil, secret, or public. God holds us accountable for how we live and serve here on earth. The judgment is future, but it deals with things past. So, the judgment connects the now and what was once future. The past was once the future, just as tomorrow will become today, and today will become yesterday.

We are spiritually lost when we depart from our created purpose and duty; it happened to Lucifer and to our ancestral parents in Eden. Upon the Fall of humans in the Paradise Garden, humankind went astray from God and became lost sheep. The incarnation of the Christ was intended to bring us back to God (Isaiah 53; John 3:14-18). For this reason, Jesus calls Himself "the good shepherd" who came to "seek and to save that which was lost" (John 10: 11-17).

When we lose vision of our purpose here, we throw away our lives because we work selfishly like the rich fool Jesus spoke about. He did get rich, but he lost it all, including his own soul to a hellish future (Luke 12:13-12). To help us focus our vision on what is of greatest importance, Jesus gives us this directive, "Seek first the kingdom of God and his righteousness and all other things will be added to you" (Matthew 6:33-34). We should make God's kingdom our priority and eternity the focus of our vision. All that you have acquired here you cannot keep; it will leave you or you will leave it.

Where are You Going from Here?

Some people have no concern about the destination of life; they have given no serious thought to it; others deliberately chose their destination and carefully plan for it. There is a third group that reflects a little but like Felix (in Acts 24:25), they defer making a choice and put off planning for a more convenient day. But that convenient day never comes.

Where am I going from here? The answer to this question points back to how well we have answered the previous three questions of identity, worth, and purpose. If we truly know ourselves as God's created beings, His image bearers, His representatives in the earth realm, and that we are here to serve Him and neighbors. Then we should also know God is preparing for us a more perfect life in a more perfect environment in the world tomorrow.

Tomorrow's world is moving toward us. It is beautifully captured in the closing chapters of the Bible, Revelation 21 and 22. This majestic world is also dealt with in volume 10 of the series, "Related Events to the Second Coming of the Christ" and is titled, *The New World Order.*[2+]

It is to this eternal destination you are now invited to register for before death seize upon you. You are invited to register by having your name inscribed in the Lamb's Book of Life in heaven, because only these registrants are granted citizenship (Revelation 21: 27). You are registered when you have a salvation relationship with Jesus Christ (John 3:16).

Different expressions are used to describe this saving relationship, such as being born again, to be saved or converted, to know Jesus as Savior and Lord. It cannot be a faked relationship; it has to be authentic (John 3:5, 16-17).

Summation

If you knew how God sees you, and how He feels about you, you would never want to be separated from Him. That knowledge should urgently move you to leap at the opportunity to complete your registration now for time and eternity.

You were created in love as God's image bearer, to represent Him in the earth realm and share the joys and riches of His kingdom for time and eternity. That is who you are, a child of God with an eternal destiny all carved out.

But something when tragically wrong; our ancestral parents were deceived and made an irreversible compromise with the archenemy of God, Satan, and we loss it all. But God did not give up on us; He pursued us in love and redeemed us in love at the high cost of the life of His one and only Son, Jesus Christ (John 3:16). By His substitutionary death and triumphant resurrection, He conquered the enemy and redeemed us back to God. But here is the legal twist.

Since our ancestral parents were created as free moral agents, and chose Satan freely, we must freely choose Jesus for our redemption to be effective. This is what we do when we register in the Lamb's Book of Life. It marks our acceptance of Jesus and eternally seals it.

You must accomplish this registration process with the help of the blessed Holy Spirit before physical death comes to you, otherwise the offer is forever off the table.

The cost of your registration is paid in full by our Lord Jesus Christ, you do not have to pay anything; the offer is God's free gift of grace to you (John 3:16; Romans 6: 23; Ephesian 2:14). The rest of this book further explains the details of this eternally generous transaction.

CHAPTER 2
THE REALITY OF
HEAVEN

We are not going to have the usual discussion about heaven here; there is a glut of material already on the market on the subject. Much of it fictional of course because the focus is on the near-death experiences of people. They claim to have died and went to heaven. Others claim to have had visions of heaven, nothing new or awe-inspiring, just ordinary stories, seemingly made up to impress simple-minded and gullible people with itching ears for such amusements. Despite that, heaven is real!

Our focus here is not the atmospheric heaven or the planetary heaven but the third heaven where God dwells. Science has overwhelmingly confirmed that the first and second heaven exist. But they are unable to confirm or deny that the third heaven exist. God has either put it so far away that not even the

James B. Webb Telescope has yet to pick it up. Or God has made it invisible to scientific equipment as He is invisible.

Of course, the Bible teaches that God is light, and He dwells in inapproachable light (1Timothy 6:16; 1John 1:5-7). But it is also true that what we know of God is by revelation; what we discover is what He chose to reveal to us. God knows the curiosity of humans; He created humans and endowed them with capabilities and set limits they cannot cross. So, using science equipment to search for God is nothing short of an exercise in futility. God has already revealed Himself in the person of Jesus Christ (John 1:1-4,14; Hebrews 1:1-4).

From Genesis to Revelation, the reality of heaven is spoken of in the Word of God. The Bible overwhelmingly presents the heavens as real places created by God (Genesis 1:1). The third heaven is where God dwells, even though He is omnipresent (Psalm 139: 7-12; Revelation 4-19).

Jesus spoke confidently of heaven and invited all His followers to heaven (John 14:1-4). All believers are awaiting the fulfillment of this promise, while recruiting others to join them.

Of all persons, Jesus should know of the reality of heaven because He is the agent and owner of all creation (Psalm 24:1; John 1:1-2; Colossians 1:15-17). He came to earth from heaven, and He returned to heaven in the face of many witnesses (John 3:13; Acts 1:9-11). Furthermore, Jesus was seen in heaven after His ascension (Acts 7:54-60; Revelation 4:1-4, 5: 6-10). Jesus will call for His people to join Him in heaven (1Thessalonians 4:16-17). Jesus will return to earth from heaven to end the Great Tribulation (Revelation 19:11-21).

In view of all this evidence on the reality of heaven, if you are still not convinced that the place is real, then persuading you of such reality is futile, and perhaps unnecessary. You need to be first persuaded to establish a relationship with Jesus Christ, because then and only then you will experience heaven as a citizen. Non-citizens will be shut out of heaven to face the eternal wrath of God Almighty (Revelation 21: 7-8).

Citizens of the Kingdom

There are a few things worth emphasizing about citizenship in heaven or in the kingdom of God. First, our heavenly citizenship is based upon our relationship with Jesus Christ. That is a salvation relationship, gifted through God's grace (John 3:16; Romans 6: 23; Ephesians 2:8-10).

If a gift is not received it is rejected. Those who reject God's gift of salvation in Jesus Christ have no citizenship in heaven and they will perish (John 3:14-18).

Second, our salvation relationship with Jesus Christ makes us children of God with inheritance rights (John 1:12-13; Romans 8: 14-17). We are not only members of God's family, we are also citizens of His kingdom through a new birth experience (John 3:5). Kingdom means king's domain; the domain that the king rules over and owns. The Universe is God's domain; He owns it by rights of creation (Psalm 24:1, 95:1-7). The people of God are co-heirs and joint-heirs with Jesus Christ to all that God owns, which is everything.

Let us come to this again. The Word of God says that Jesus Christ is the only begotten Son of God, the Father. That means, there is no one equal to Jesus. He is in a category all by Himself (John 3:16 KJV). We who are born again children of God are adopted into God's family, and we share the inheritance with

Jesus our brother. As a child of God and registrant of heaven, you are entitled to all that God has; that is what you sign up for.

Third, it is God the Father who qualifies us for our heavenly inheritance (James 2:5). Bear in mind that God's program of redemption is to shape all humans who come to Him in the image of His Son and guarantee them citizenship in heaven with an inheritance. The implication is that some people will not deliberately choose heaven as their eternal destination; they will take the default choice instead. For that reason, they have no citizenship in heaven. Concerning such people, the apostle Paul gives us the following intelligence report:

> Their destiny is destruction, their god is their stomach, and their glory is in their shame. Their mind is set on earthly things. But our citizenship is in heaven. And we eagerly await a Savior from there, the Lord Jesus Christ, who, by the power that enables him to bring everything under his control, will transform our lowly bodies so that they will be like his glorious body. (Philippians 3:19-21)

The apostle Peter affirms that through the redemptive works of Jesus Christ, believers are not only made citizens of the Kingdom of God, but they also have been given an "inheritance incorruptible and undefiled and that does not fade away reserved [in heaven for them]" (1Peter 1: 3-5 NKJV). The inheritance is guaranteed in the will, God's covenant (Hebrews 9:15-28).

Fourth, in the final two chapters of Revelation (21-22) heaven and earth are redefined because both are recreated and enjoined and God has relocated to dwell with His people.

The capital city of the world tomorrow is the New Jerusalem of Revelation 21:9-27. It is a city built in heaven by heavenly architects and descends out of heaven as the new dwelling place of God and His people. This City of God will be suspended over the new earth and is accessible from the four the regions of the new earth through twelve gates that are never closed (for more on this read *The New World Order*, volume10 in the series by this author entitled, "Related Events to the Second Coming of the Christ").[1]

The Kingdom of God

The believers' citizenship and inheritance fall in the context of the Kingdom of God. In other words, citizenship and inheritance are connected to geography or place, real property. The Bible is about a King and His kingdom. God's Kingdom is the entire Universe. It is so large the greater part of it is invisible to our naked eyes. God created earth as the dwelling place for humans, a specie He created in His own image and is transforming them to rule eternally as His extended family.

There are two dimensions to the kingdom of God: the spiritual and the material. The material is territorial; it is the domain over which the King rules or exercises authority. The spiritual is the rule or the exercise of authority itself. When Americans elect a President, they give authority to one person to exercise rule over them in a defined geography called, the United States of America. God is not elected or appointed, but He exercises ultimate rule over the Universe, including the heavens and the earth.

Humans are free moral agents, created by God. God is Almighty and can compel every being to serve Him. But He has chosen not to rule over humans by force, because force would be counter-productive to the exercise of free will. And it would not bring Him genuine glory. Therefore, God has chosen to win the hearts of humans by love, mercy, and compassion (Psalm 103:1-19; John 3:16). A parent who receives a voluntary kiss from a child before leaving for school in the mornings has a greater sense of satisfaction than the parent who pays the child for the kiss. A paid kiss is forced and therefore not genuine.

God's plan of redemption is His attempt to win humans inwardly by exercising His love (John 3:16). The incarnation is not God showing up on earth in all His power, splendor, and majesty to force humans to fall to their knees and worship Him. No! The incarnation is God laying aside His glory, divesting Himself of His riches and majesty to become one of us in the person of Jesus Christ (John 1:1-5, 14; Philippians 2:5-11).

Jesus was not born in the palace of a king, in the elite section of town. He was born in a manger and grew up in the humble village of Nazareth (Luke 2:1-20; Matthew 2:19-23). His message was about the kingdom of God, loving and serving your neighbor. His demonstration of authentic love was to surrender His life redemptively on a cross. God came down to us in the person of Jesus Christ and won our hearts by love (John 3:16).

For these reasons, Jesus preached that the kingdom of God is in you; that the kingdom of God is among you, and he taught us to pray for the kingdom to come (Matthew 6: 9).

In His first advent, Jesus did not seek to rule from the throne of King David or Ceasar's throne but to rule from the citadel of the human heart. He came to win us inwardly by the sacrifice of Himself; that is the highest form of love. "Greater love has no one than this: to lay down one's life for one's friends" (John

15:13). We were not even His friends; we were His enemies when he lay down His life for our redemption.

Because He was unwilling to use His supernatural powers to launch a Barabbas-like revolution against Rome and restore the Jewish State, the religious elite framed Jesus and pressured the Roman Governor to execute an innocent man (John 18: 28-19:1-16). The high priest Caiaphas not only led the crowd to shout crucify Him; he threatened the position of the governor when he said, "If you let this man go, you are not Caesar's friend." He claims to be a king, "We have no king, but Caesar" (John 19:7, 14-16). For political expediency, Pilate capitulated.

They got what they wanted an execution of Jesus of Nazareth. They hung Him high and stretched Him wide on a Roman cross perched on a hill called Calvary. There He died between two thieves (John 19:16-18). They meant it for evil, but God meant it for good. God used it to redeem humankind in love. One poet expresses it in song with these words, "When I got a glimpse of true love, it was hanging from an old rugged cross."

When Jesus returns, He will sit on the throne of King David in the earthly Jerusalem in Israel and rule over the earth in righteousness (Isaiah 9:6-7). This is called the millennial reign of the Christ (Revelation 20:1-10).[2] Believers will reign over the earth with Him, but this is not the full manifestation of the kingdom that we pray to come in the Lord's prayer.

After the millennium and the final judgment, there will be a new heaven, a new earth and a new capital city, the New Jerusalem, which constitutes the New World Order. Here we will see the full manifestation of the Kingdom of God in all its glory. Here God and His people will reign eternally. For more on these themes, see Volumes 7, 9, and 10 in the series, "Related Events to the Second Coming of the Christ" by this author.[3]

Summation

We have seen that in addition to the atmospheric heaven and the planetary heaven, there is a third heaven where God dwells. The entire Universe is His kingdom; He created it, owns it, and exercises governance over it. But there is also a spiritual domain over which God exercises rule as well. That domain is the human heart, the interior kingdom. It is a more difficult place to rule.

Humans are created as free moral agents, in the image of God, with the power of reason and choice. God does not exercise rule over them by force because that would bring Him no quality or sincere glory. God wins over humans by lovingkindness and sacrificial love as the incarnation demonstrates.

God became man in the person of Jesus Christ and offered Himself on a cross in love; their redemption is the highest form of sacrificial love (John 3:16; Roman 5:1-11).

All humans who respond to God's love in Jesus Christ will live and reign with Him not only in the millennial kingdom of Jesus Christ but in the New World Order (Revelation 21-22).

The registration of which this book speaks, is the act of you signing up to inherit all this, by having a salvation relationship with Jesus Christ now (John 3:16). The time to get registered is short; death and the coming of the Lord can happen anytime.

CHAPTER 3

THE
NECESSITY OF HELL

Like heaven, we are not having the usual discussion about the existence of hell. We are not going to debate whether hell exist or not, or try to determine its location, or how a loving, compassionate, and benevolent God could allow anyone to go to hell. There are numerous volumes already in print on these issues. The Word of God is clear on the subject and that stands.

Whether we believe in the existence of heaven or hell does not change the reality of their existence and our accountability to God. We must face Him and one of these realms or locations will be our eternal destination.

Hell is a real place and many of us humans are at risk going there, if we refuse to accept God's provision of salvation. I would be doing you a disservice to write about the joys of heaven and say nothing about hell. In this chapter, therefore, I will first touch on the reality of hell, then discuss briefly why hell is necessary.

One woman said to me, I do not believe in hell! I responded, Mom, I am not asking you to believe in hell. I am asking you to believe in Jesus; He is your life jacket to save you from hell. If you were going on a cruise, and they said to you, this ship is so large, it is unsinkable. For that reason, there is no need to carry lifeboats. My advice would be, cancel your vacation; it is not safe! This could be Titanic 2.0!

The Reality of Hell

First, the Word of God in both Testaments, directly speaks of hell frequently and in numerous passages (Psalm 9:17; Deuteronomy 32: 22 KJV). Different words are used to refer to this underworld place; at times, the grave. In Hebrew it is called *Sheol,* in Greek *Hades.*[1] The word *Gehenna* is also used for hell, a place of burning.

*Paradis*e or Abraham's bosom seems to have had close geography to hell, but not a place of torment according to Jesus. The wicked, rich man in hell was able to see the poor man, Lazarus, in *Paradise* (Luke 16:19-26). So, it is a place, even if .located in another realm other than the underworld.[2]

The fire of hell is what many people are concerned about, but fire is used symbolically. In the physical, fire for us torments, it burns. But people who go to hell will not be going there in their physical body but in their resurrection body (John 5:28).

34

The Bible tells us, "As in Adam all die, even so in Christ shall all be made alive" (1 Corinthians 15:22). Fire as we know it cannot do any harm to the resurrection body because it is not a physical body; it is a spiritual body. At the resurrection believers get a body suited for heaven, and unbelievers get a body suited for their destination (1 Corinthians 15:35-58). So, we should not think of hell as fire as we know it or think of the body as physical; like cremation, a physical body would be ashes in a few minutes. Hell is something far worse than physical.

R.C. Sproul used three expressions to represent hell, "The place of God's disfavor," the place of "the great separation," and the place which is "the point of no return." Sproul asserts that we are dealing with symbolical language that points to a reality of torment far beyond what we humans can imagine.[3]

Jesus went to Paradise immediately after death; He went with one of the thieves who died with him and the cross (Luke 23:39-42). If His visit was to the righteous in *Paradise*, then those in hell could hear Him speak, so they hear again the salvation they rejected by not listening to Moses and the prophets of their day (1Peter 1:18-20; 2 Peter 2:4-9).

It is believed that *Paradise* was located in an underworld compartment where the righteous souls went after death, but upon Jesus' visit, it was transferred to heaven at His resurrection or at His ascension (Matthew 27:50-52; Ephesians 4:7-10).[4]

But in this chapter, I am referring to the lake of burning sulfur, the place of final and eternal punishment for both Satan, his angels, and unregenerate humans of which Jesus and His apostles refer (Revelation 20:11-15). Satan and his angels are spirit beings that no fire as we known can harm. Unbelievers will be given a body suitable for this same destination.

35

There is no getting around the authority of Scripture through clever arguments. There are those who appeal to the love of God; to them God is so loving, He will not send anyone to hell. In substance, they are saying, God cannot enforce His own law.

Yet, the very verse of Scripture that tells us God loves us to the point of sacrificing His Son to save us, also tells us why God did it. He did it "that we might not perish but have eternal life (John 3:16). Why would God go to such extreme to save us, if there were not something eternally awful, He is saving us from.

Second, Jesus the Son of God speaks vividly and extensively of hell. In Matthew 13:41-43 Jesus declares that at the end of the age, the Son of Man will send His holy angels to gather the wicked like stubble for burning and throw them in to hell. Again, He uses language familiar to His hearers to point to a reality far beyond their imagination.

In Matthew 13:47-50, Jesus liken the kingdom of heaven to a fisherman's net thrown into the sea for a catch, and when drawn, it brings to shore all kinds of marine life. He sought what he wanted and throws back the rejects into the sea. In the same manner, the wicked will be separated from the righteous at the end of the age. And the wicked will the thrown into the fire where there will be "weeping and gnashing of teeth."

Jesus describes hell a place where the fire is not quenched, and the worms do not die (Mark 9:43-48). What does that mean? The body is not consumed as in cremation and there is no let up or pause to the suffering. Even if Jesus was referring to a local garbage dump where refuse were constantly burning, He used it to illustrate the existence of a real place of eternality that humans who reject God's grace will finally go.

Jesus further speaks of a broad way that leads to destruction that many have entered upon and a narrow way that leads to life that few find (Matthew 7:13-14). The narrow way is not hidden from anyone. It represents the righteous lifestyle that places demands upon all of us. It is a disciplined path or lifestyle. For this reason, it is unattractive to some people, and so they reject it, even though it leads to eternal life.

People want heaven but they want it on their own terms, so they ignore God's way to get there for their own way. They want to say, "I did it my way" as the popular song goes. But our way is most often the wrong way; it is not God's way (Isaiah 55:8-10). The Word of God has not kept us in the dark concerning the joys of heaven and the dangers of hell. God has made provision how to gain one and avoid the other.

Third, the apostles of Jesus speak about hell and warned against this awful place, as a place to be avoided (1 Peter 3:19; 2 Peter 2:9). Hell was not created for humans; it was created for rebels, Satan, and his angels. Humans who join the cause of the rebels will end up where the rebels end up, prison.

In this world, if you join rebels to burglarize a bank or join the insurrection on the capital, you are a rebel and will go to prison with the rebels after due process. The kingdom of God operates similarly. It has a judicial system that enforces justice.

Fourth, people are not thrown into hell without due process. The Final Judgment is the Supreme Court of God Almighty in session. It will first be in session as the Believers' Judgment, then as the Judgment of Nations including Israel, then the Final Judgment. It is evidence based, that is why books are opened and people are judged according to what is on record about them in the books (Jude 6-7; Revelation 20:12-15).[5]

God Is Just and Merciful

First, hell is necessary because God is just. A just society is governed by laws faithfully executed without partiality. If Hitler did not kill himself, is there any just court on earth that would have let him off the hook for his atrocities? I hardly think so!

But why is that? Because humans have a moral sense of fairness and justice. And where did they get that sense of justice and respect for human life? They God it from the Word of God (Exodus 20:1-17; Deuteronomy 5:6-21). Western jurisprudence is built upon the Hebrew/Christian Bible, the Word of God. So, the Bible came from the Middle East to the West. All this is common knowledge.

Additionally, humans have this biblical sense of justice because they are the image bearer of God, and the moral law of God is inside of them (Genesis 1:26-27; Jeremiah 31:31-37).

And what will God do with Hitler and other wicked humans at the judgment? Just wink at them and throw heavens' gate open and let these unrepentant murderers in? I do not think so! And if you think so, you do not know the God of the Bible. His Son would have died in vain, and he would not be the God of justice and mercy of Scripture.

The wicked, whether they be humans or devils, will be given due process and sent to the destination they have chosen for themselves. Everyone that goes to hell, goes by choice; they may later regret their choice, but which man facing the gallows does not regret his choice? But that does not reverse justice.

Second, hell is necessary because God is holy. The darkness of sin and evil is completely antithetical to God's nature (1John 1:5-7). God must rid His creation of everything that goes contrary to His holy nature. Sin in God's creation is worse than a malignant cancer to the human body. The physician who will declare the person healthy must first eradicate all cancer from the body. God will do exactly that and create all things new.

God's new heaven and earth will not be tainted with the malignancies of the old order because He will completely eradicate evil from His creation, including Satan himself, and create all things new (Revelation 21:1-5).

Third, Hell is necessary because God is merciful. This one will throw you, and you are likely to exclaim, what! It seems a bit illogical so, let us unpack this a little. Because God is all-powerful, He does not give us humans exactly what we deserve. He restrains justice by mercy and calls for mercy in human relationships (Micah 6:8; Matthew 5:7).

Hell was not created for humans as previously stated. It was created for the worst enemy God has in His universe, a rebel called, Satan, including his angels. Satan is opposed to God's holy nature and character. Hell is the appropriate punishment set up from the beginning for this rebel and his followers. God cannot change that outcome for the rebel and remain true to Himself. Humans are given many chances to be rescued, but some will not be rescued because they refuse God's mercy.

For example, when God created man, He enacted a law that brings death if violated. God's mercy is shown in four ways:

1) God made it easy for the man and his wife to obey His executive order by giving them full disclosure of the one tree they should stay away from, and the consequence they would suffer if they disobeyed. Adam and Eve cannot say they sinned ignorantly. In the light of full disclosure, they made a willful choice to follow Satan.

2) God showed them mercy by not taking their lives promptly, though the effects of death was already in their

body; He took the life of an animal instead, thus giving them redemption on credit until the Redeemer comes. God used the skin of the animal to cover their nakedness. This signals that only a righteousness provided by God can adequately cover sinful humans. All this point to e Redeemer Jesus Christ (Genesis 3: 15, 21; John1:29).

3) He expelled them from the garden, so they could not eat from the tree of life and live forever in their sinful state of death and dying; that would have been hell for the entire human family. Expelling them was an act of mercy (Genesis 3:21-24). Suffering without dying is hell.

4) Since the entire human race was in Adam, the effects of the poison fruit he and his wife ingested was passed on to Adam's posterity (Romans 5:12). The seed of death they ingested was transmitted to the entire human race. But God made them a promise to send His Son to save the entire human family from eternal death (Genesis 3:15; John 3:16). Jesus is the antidote to the poison our ancestral parents ingested in the Paradise Garden.

Any human being that rejects this antidote of redemption that cost God the life of His Son is saying to God, my choice is with Satan. All humans who join Satan's enterprise against God will go with Satan and his angels to the eternal place of banishment prepared for them.

God's mercy is demonstrated in His plan of redemption. Humans are the only beings in God's creation that are the beneficiaries of redemption. Redemption is a rescue mission for humans only. Anyone who refuses to be rescued will perish (John 3:16). The Word of God has made that fact clear. It tells us as in Adam all die, even so in Christ shall all be made alive. And that "the wages of sin is death, but the gift of God is eternal life through Jesus Christ our Lord" (Romans 6:23).

Fourth, hell is necessary because every kingdom or nation State has a judicial and law enforcement system. The concept of family and nation find their origin in God (Genesis 1:26-28, 12:1-3). The Kingdom of God is the primary example of law making and law enforcement (Genesis 2:15-17, 3:8-24, 4:8-16). God is the King of the Universe and the original lawgiver (Exodus 20:1-17).

Fifth, hell is necessary because the wicked must get their just due and the innocent must be vindicated. This is why Jesus is called "the righteous judge" by Saint Paul (2 Timothy 4:8). There are people who have had their lives taken, their property confiscated by the powerful; they had never seen justice in this life. But there is a day of reckoning coming when the Righteous Judge will vindicate the cause of the innocent.

A Righteous Government

Earth has never seen a righteous government, but one is coming. The Prophet Isaiah informs us that the Messiah, Jesus Christ will head up such a government that is predicated on righteousness, peace, justice, and unprecedented prosperity He said:

> For to us a child is born, to us a son is given, and the government will be on his shoulders. And he will be called Wonderful Counselor, Mighty God, Everlasting Father, Prince of Peace. Of the greatness of his government and peace there shall be no end. He will reign on David's throne and over his kingdom,

establishing and upholding it with justice and righteousness from that time on and forever. The zeal of the Lord Almighty will accomplish this. (Isa. 9: 6-7)

The preceding Scripture verse speaks of the Millennium when Jesus will reign from the earthly Jerusalem in Israel, fulfilling certain promises to that nation. But He will be King over all the earth, and Savior and Lord for all peoples dwelling on the earth.

Satan will be in prison during this time of the Millennium, but he will still have some diehard followers that keep his enterprise going (Revelation 20:1-3, 7-10). To fully understand the unfolding of prophetic history up to this time and beyond, read all ten volumes by this author, series, "Related Events to the Second Coming of the Christ."

The Millennium will last for a thousand years, and after it there will be the Final Judgment that will do away with Satan and his angels, death and hades, sickness, and disease, and all evil in the creation (Revelation 20:11-15).

After the Final Judgment comes the New World Order with a new heaven and a new earth, and the New Jerusalem which is the Universal Capital and dwelling place of God and Christ, and His people.

It is to all this that humans are invited to register now. You name must be registered in the Book of Life before physical death comes to you.[6] If your name is not in the Book of Life, it is in the default registry known as "the books" (Revelation 20:11-15). I call these books, "the books of wrath."[7] You do well accepting God's offer and salvation and getting your name in the Book of Life in heaven; it is the book that truly matters in the end.

Summation

In this chapter, the reality and necessity of hell are briefly discussed. The Word of God, Jesus and the apostles and the early church all considered hell and heaven as real places created by God for specific purposes. The third heaven is the dwelling place of God. Hell is part of God's Kingdom; it falls in the judicial and law enforcement branch of His government.

On the necessity of hell, five points are given to make the case. The fundamental ones are the justice of God, the holiness of God, and the mercy of God.

Hell was not created for humans but for the devil and his angels. But humans who refused God's rescue plan of redemption and join with the devil against God will earn for themselves the same destination as the devil.

Hell is fundamentally about human choice and God's justice. The burning fire of hell is not about physical or natural burning as we know it but something far worse. Hell is about the disfavor of God, separation from His graciousness, eternal banishment from all that is good. People end up in hell because they refused to be rescued (John 3:16).

A drowning man who refused to be rescued will in the end be a drowned man. Humans are free moral agents; we are free to choose who we want to rule over us. But choices have rewards and consequences. Eternal life is the reward, and eternal death is the consequence (John 3:16; 5:28).

The Book of Life is where you want your name to be on the day of judgment. To guarantee that you must register now, before you exit the physical body at death.

HEAVEN *If You Want In* **REGISTER NOW!**

CHAPTER 4

THE WAY TO HEAVEN

The way to heaven is also referred to as the way to life or eternal life, or the way to enter the kingdom of heaven or the kingdom of God. In this chapter, we will include these references. But we will first look at a few misconceptions.

Misconceptions of how you get to heaven are numerous and dangerous. Dangerous because most of them give people a false sense of security. People think they are okay on their way to heaven only to learn later that the path they have taken does not lead to heaven; it terminates somewhere else, and it is not good.

If you find out at the end of life that you took the wrong path, then it is too late for you. Your destination cannot be changed when you die; there is no going back to take the right path. For that reason, this chapter invites you to examine closely the path you are on, because many are mistaken, and you do not need to be one of them. Jesus made it clear that not everyone who calls Him Lord will enter the kingdom but those who do the will of His Father (Matthew 7:21-23).

Even though there are only two eternal destinations, people have great difficulty making the right choice. One fundamental reason for the difficulty is that people want to get to heaven on their own terms. That position is completely untenable. Think of heaven as a foreign country with its own sovereignty and laws, you cannot write the terms by which you get in. The government of that country set the terms that gives entrance to foreigners. You must first know the terms and abide by them closely if you wish to gain entrance. The same is true of heaven.

Some of the misconceptions discussed in this chapter are my attempt to point you, the reader, to the one right way to heaven. Misconceptions are broadly held, and they are deceptive as a counterfeit dollar bill. You must look carefully to uncover these deceptions by comparing what is offered to the Word of God. Heaven is God's dwelling place; He sets the terms of entry, not you or me.

Common Misconception About Heaven

The first misconception is, there are many paths to heaven. The argument says, heaven is like a mountain, there are many paths leading to its summit, but once you get there, all will have the same view. In this case all the religions, cults, and worship systems in the world would be paths to heaven. It does not take much to see the absurdity of such a view.

The many paths theory may be true of a mountain, but certainly not true of heaven. The notion of many paths to heaven is not biblical; it suits those who want to get to heaven on their own terms. But there is hardly a country on earth that a foreigner can enter on his or her own terms, much more heaven, God's holy abode. The many paths theory is wishful thinking that will most certainly land its adherents in the place of eternal destruction.

Jesus said broad is the way to destruction and many enter there upon. And narrow is the way to life, and few find it. A broad way speaks of many paths or a liberal lifestyle. A narrow way speaks of a singular path, a disciplined lifestyle (Matthew 7:13-14). Jesus told Nicodemus that he must be born again to enter the kingdom of God (John 3:1-5). God sets the terms.

Second misconception. This asserts that you get to heaven by being a morally good person. On the surface, this notion seems logical and reasonable. But again, it is not biblical.

People often say, "I live a clean life." "I am honest; I don't defraud people." "I pay my taxes." "My hands are not in any iniquity; I am a good person; I don't see what would prevent me from going to heaven." In truth, by this world's standard there are many good people, and they sincerely believe that their personal goodness merits them a place in God's heaven. But again, they are so wrong!

By God's standard of righteousness, there is no good person outside of Jesus Christ. "All have sinned and come short of the glory of God. There is none righteous, no not one" (Romans 3:9-12). We human are sinners by nature; our self-righteousness are filthy rags in the sight of God. For this reason, repentance from sin is a first step requirement for acceptance to the kingdom of God (Luke 24: 45-49; Acts 2:36-41). In other words, a spiritually transformed life is required (John 3:5; Romans 12:1-2).

The third misconception. Good works will qualify me for a place in God's heaven. This group holds to the philosophy that on the Day of Judgment, if your good deeds outweigh your bad deeds, you will be given the rite of passage to enter heaven.

Again, this sounds reasonable, but it is found nowhere in the Bible where you can enter heaven on the merit of your good works. Good works cannot be a substitute for a born-again relationship with Jesus Christ. If it could, the following story would have been totally unnecessary.

Cornelius, a Roman centurion was a philanthropist, and a good man by this world's standard. Heaven took note of his generosity, but it was not enough to get him into the kingdom of God. God through an angel instructed Cornelius to call for the apostle Peter to explain the way of salvation to Cornelious and his family. Peter came to Cornelius' house, preached Christ, and the Holy Spirit came upon all of them. Peter then baptized them in water (Acts 10:1-48).

Do not underestimate the place for good works in the kingdom of God. Here is the distinction we must make: we do not do good works to get into the kingdom, but once we are in the kingdom, good works are required; they are a natural outcome. Life in Christ is a productive life (John 15:1-7; Ephesian 2, 4:2). Believers will be rewarded for their good works offered to Christ (2 Corinthians 5:10).[1]

The bottom line is this—you should practice being a good person and doing good works, but good works cannot be offered to God as a substitute for salvation. It will not get you into heaven (John 3:5). God has prescribed the way to heaven and no created being can change it. Good works is not it!

The Fourth misconception. If I am baptized and become a member of a church, I will surely get into heaven. This is a widespread conviction that people have, and it is very dangerous. It is dangerous because they are two necessary requirements when we come into relationship with Christ, but they cannot stand alone; there are other requirements.

For that reason, you do not get baptized to be saved; you get baptized because you are saved, you already have a relationship with Jesus Christ. Some people had the ritual done, but they never repented of their sins, received God's forgiveness, and experienced the new birth. They had no transforming experience of redeeming grace. And for that reason, they have a false sense of security; they think they are saved, but they are not.

Church membership given without repentance gives the same false sense of security. A person must be born again before he or she is baptized in water and given the right hand of fellowship to be a church member. Only born-again people are given entrance into the kingdom of God; they are the ones who are registered in heaven in the Lamb's book of life (John 3:1-7; Hebrews 12:22-24).

There are several examples of this in scripture we could cite, but only two are given here. First, Simon Magus, the sorcerer of Samaria. At the preaching of the gospel by Evangelist Philip, Simon surrendered his magic arts paraphernalia, got baptized and join the church. But it was later discovered that the man had not truly repented with a relationship with Jesus Christ. Peter rebuked him when he offered money to buy the power of the blessed Holy Spirit (Acts 8:1-24).

The next example is "The Rich Young Ruler." He was a deeply devoted man in his Jewish faith, but he was spiritually empty. This aching void brought him to Jesus. He asked Jesus what can he do to inherit eternal life.

Jesus told him to part with his wealth and come follow him. But he went away sorrowful because his wealth held him too fast. In today's evangelical church, he would be an ideal candidate for membership. He knew the Hebrew Scripture, he was young, a community leader of status, and he was rich.

These are popular misconceptions but by themselves will not get you into heaven and I will tell you why.

- A whole nation has been there and done that, and it has not and will not get them into heaven by themselves. Jesus considered them lost and offered them salvation first, but they rejected him (John 1:12).
- The law was weak; it could not save them (Romans 8:3). Animal sacrifice by themselves could not save them (Hebrews 10:1-7).
- The rich young ruler experienced the emptiness of religion without Jesus. He came to Jesus to remedy the situation but walked away empty because his riches got in the way (Luke 18:18-25).
- On the day of judgment, preachers, pastors, and many others will present their ministry work and religious practices as reasons to get into heaven and will be turned away.

Fifth misconception. The only requirement is keeping the Ten Commandments, do the best you can. Jesus died for the entire world anyway. All will be saved (John 3:16).

No one has been able to keep the Law of God; if you break one you break all (James 2:8-11). If those to whom it was first given had kept it, there would have been no need for a new covenant or law (Hebrews 8: 7-13). The New Covenant is not based upon external works but upon God's grace inwardly.

Furthermore, it is written inwardly, and the blessed Holy Spirit is given to assist us to do right (Roman 8:1-16). Jesus is the only one to perfectly fulfill the law of God.

It is true, therefore, that Jesus died for all humankind, but a careful reading of John 3:16 includes the words, "that whosoever believes in him should not perish but have eternal life." The verse divides humankind into two camps: believers and unbelievers. Believers get eternal life, unbelievers perish.

Sixth misconception. If you are religious, you will enter heaven. There are many religions in this world and most if not all, are religions of "salvation." Commonly used, salvation means deliverance, deliverance from something, anything. In that context, they seek to improve human lives to one measure or another. Christianity is much different.

In biblical Christianity, salvation means deliverance from sin through the sacrifice of Jesus Christ, the Lamb of God (John 1:29; Romans 5:1-12). The dimension of a specific sacrifice cannot be overemphasized; it is provided by God Himself.

In this case there is no other and no equal sacrifice. Jesus Christ is the substitutionary sacrifice that ransoms humans from sin and eternal death. It is the sacrifice that serves as the full atonement for our sins and reconciles us to God (Isaiah 53; Romans 5:1-5; 2 Corinthians 5:11-21).

Additionally, the sacrifice of Jesus Christ provides the righteousness that covers us from wrath before God; it is the righteousness that God accepts. In that context, Jesus is the believers" Passover Lamb" (1Corinthian 5:7). The apostle John reminds us that Jesus is the "propitiation" or covering "for our sins" and that of the "whole world" (1John 3:1-2).

In his classic poem set to music by William B. Bradbury, Edward Mote penned these immortal words that captures the believers' standing before God at the end of the age:

> When He shall come with trumpet sound, O may I
> then in Him be found, Dressed in His Righteousness
> alone, Faultless to stand before the throne.

Our self-righteousness may be good in our own sight, but not good enough to cover us before God and shelters us from divine wrath. God alone provides the righteousness that covers us and shields us from eternal judgment.

The Way to Heaven

There is only one way to heaven, and that one way is through Jesus Christ our Lord (Acts 4:12). That truth is the focus of this section. The Word of God, the Bible is the only sure, authentic, and authoritative word on how to get to heaven. It is the inspired and inerrant Word of God. There is not another document on earth that is more trustworthy in the truth it affirms.

If you think you have found a more reliable document than the Bible that you want to trust, you will be playing Russian roulette with your life if you trust it to lead you to heaven; it will not! If the Bible does not affirm it, it is not reliable; it does not matter who writes it or who says it.

Let me say it up front, the Word of God presents Jesus Christ as the one and only way to heaven. The Word of God affirms that truth repeatedly. Let us look at a few here:

First, Jesus said He is the way to God and heaven (John 14:1-6). In this passage, Jesus talks about returning to His Father in heaven. And that He was going ahead to prepare a place for His disciples who would follow later. Disciples are not limited to the twelve men who were in the immediate company of Jesus, but to all believers of the ages. Heaven is promised to all who are in a saving relationship with Jesus Christ

Thomas, one of the disciples asked, how do we get to heaven? Jesus responded that He is the way to heaven, and He will call for them at the appropriate time. Jesus returned to heaven forty days after His resurrection with a promise to come again (Acts 1:9-11). Jesus did not set a specific time when He will return, but it will be in the context of many signs and events among and within nations. There will also be cosmic anomalies, and upheavals in nature (Matthew 24:1-51).

Before Jesus left for heaven, He gave His followers a global assignment to preach the gospel and make disciples of all nations (Matthew 28:19-10; Acts 1:8). The implication is that the gospel message must reach all nations of the world before He calls for His people (Matthew 24:14). Once He calls for His people, their assignment to preach the gospel to the nations ends.

The apostle Paul and the other apostles affirm that Jesus will first call for His people to join Him in heaven (1Corinthians 15:50-58; 1Thessalonians 4:16-18). This event is called the rapture.[2] (See the reference to learn more about the rapture).

It may seem odd to you that Jesus is the one and only way to heaven. But in fact, one way is less confusing than many! There are so many religions claiming to be the right way, but the proof they offer is not a compelling foundation for eternal life and heaven to rest on. The leaders of the various non-Christian religious movements have not claimed to be God Almighty, the Creator of heaven and earth. They never lived a sinless life, and they are all dead and remain dead.

Jesus offers the most compelling and credible credentials and is most qualified to serve as the way to heaven. He came from heaven to earth and has publicly returned to heaven, being seen by at least 120 individuals (Acts 1:9-11,14-17). He is the Son of God, the Creator and Owner of heaven and earth (Psalm 24:1; John 1:1-18; Colossians 1:15-20).

The apostle Paul further demonstrates that the Second Person of the blessed Holy Trinity pre-existed with God the Father, laid aside His glory, divested Himself of His Majesty, took upon Himself the form of a servant and surrendered His life for the redemption of humans. He rose again from the dead, ascended to heaven, and is now seated at the right hand of the Majesty on high as the High Priest over His Church. He is the only mediator between God and men (Philippians 2:5-11; Hebrews 1:1-4).

Jesus, the Gate to the Kingdom (John 10:1-29).

Jesus claims to be many things: bread of life, water of life, good shepherd, the resurrection and the life, the way, the truth, and the life, to name a few. Most of these statements are figure of speech explaining a reality about the Kingdom of God.

In this section we look at the sheepfold as a metaphor used for the kingdom of God (John 10). Jesus talks about the good shepherd, the sheep, and the sheepfold. He is the Good Shepherd. His people are the sheep, and the kingdom the

54

sheepfold. Bear in mind that His preaching and teachings were about the kingdom of heaven or the kingdom of God.

To gain entrance to the kingdom, a person must come through Jesus Christ (John 14:5-6). Note the main points in the dialogue. First, Jesus is the Good Shepherd, nobody cares about the people of God as Jesus. He is not a hired hand like the Scribes and Pharisees. He is the owner of the sheep; he offered up His life defending and protecting them.

Second, there is one sheepfold and many sheep, but they are all known by the shepherd, and they know the shepherd; they recognize His voice. This means the relationship between Jesus and His people is personal, intimate, and lasting.

Third, there is one gate to the sheepfold. This means there is one entrance to the kingdom of God. Jesus said, He is the gate; He is that entrance. This claim is consistent with Jesus' other teachings about Himself and His kingdom. For example, Jesus said He is the door (Revelation 3:8).

Fourth, the porter to the sheepfold represents the Holy Spirit. We do not want to over explain the figure of speech, but we do know that the Holy Spirit is the one who convicts people, reveals Christ, and brings them to Him to be saved. A person cannot bypass Jesus and get into heaven according to the Word of God (John 3:16-19).

No one has the authority to over-rule the Word of God. It is foolish therefore, for a person to look at the Biblical requirement and say, I do not believe that! Then offer what he thinks is a reasonable, fair, and loving way to get into heaven. The way to heaven is simple, a small child can understand it (John 3:16).

One of the reasons the Jewish religious leaders in the time of Christ rejected Him, is the fact that they did not believe Messiah to be a divine being. When He claimed to be the Son of God and able to forgive sins, they charged Him with blasphemy. When Iesus told them that He was here to set them free and open their eyes, they took that to be an insult. They pushed back by asserting that they were Abraham's seed and were never in bondage to anyone. And they were the leaders of the blind because they had the holy Scripture, the revelation of God. The fact is their own Scripture spoke of Jesus and pointed to Him; He is the fulfillment of the Hebrew Scripture. He came as their salvation from sin, the righteousness that God provides.

Therefore, rejecting Jesus is to reject their own salvation and the righteousness that would get them into heaven. Paul said, the righteousness of God unto salvation is in the gospel (Roman 1:16-17). They rejected that and went about establishing their own righteousness (Romans 10:1-5). In other words, they are inventing a path into the sheepfold of their own, they are climbing over the walls rather than come through the one gave which is Jesus Christ (John 14:6; Acts 4:12).

The irony is—there are some evangelicals today who do not think Jews have to come to Jesus to be saved, so they play down witnessing to them. Some of them have moved their ministry offices to Israel, not to get Jews saved, but to provide social programs. They ask the rest of us to stand with Israel by sending money to support those social programs.

This book is not saying supporting social programs is wrong, but to do it to the neglect of the saving of the soul is seriously heretical. Every person, Jew or Gentile who dies without acknowledging Jesus as Savior and Lord is lost; they have missed heaven. The Bible does not teach a path to heaven outside of a saving relationship with Jesus Christ.

CHAPTER 5

HOW TO REGISTER FOR HEAVEN

Registration in the kingdom of God is a human and divine process; you have a role to play, and God has a role to play. First, God wants you and me in His kingdom and so He did the heavy lifting on our behalf to make it possible. Left to ourselves, we would not choose God or heaven.

Second, Jesus invites us to come to Him for salvation and thereby exchange our heavy burdens for His light one. He said, "My yoke is easy, and my burden is light" (Matthew 11:28-20). In other words, God provides Himself an acceptable sacrifice for our redemption. That sacrifice is Jesus Christ, our Lord (John 3:16). There is no other sacrifice acceptable to God for the redemption of humans apart from Jesus Christ.

God's love is amazing and relentless. We as sheep gone astray have been pursued by the Good Shepherd who gave His life for us in a rescue mission called, redemption (Isaiah 53:6-12; Romans 5:11). Symbolically, as the ram caught in the tickets on Mount Mariah was offered by Abraham in Isaac's place, so Jesus was offered in our place (Genesis 22:1-19). It was God who provided the ram for Abraham, and it was God who offered His Son for us on Mount Calvary (John 3:16).

This decision to redeem humans was made in the Godhead from eternity past but carried out in time on Calvary (Galatians 4:4-5; Revelation 13:8). We come to God through Christ. God chose us to be His children long before we were born (Ephesians 1:4-7). God also carries out the work of justification and shares in the work of sanctification (Romans 8:33; 1Thess.5:23).

The human side of our registration in heaven is wrapped up in the seven steps discussed in the following section. This includes our responsibility to grow in our faith to Christian maturity. Our registration to heaven's *Book of Life* begins with a relationship with Jesus Christ. That relationship has a starting point but no ending point; it is life long and eternal.

As long as you are alive in your physical body, this relationship will Jesus Christ will be in place, unless you voluntarily cancels it. And even so, cancellation is not easy because you are not likely to cancel a good thing as eternal life. God will not cancel, and no one else can. Those that are chosen by God are the ones that are called, sanctified, justified, and continue to glorification (Romans 8:29-39).

So, if you are truly born again, not even death can break the bond between you and Jesus Christ. When your physical body changes from mortal to immortal, the relationship continues; this is the eternal life aspect of the union (John 3:16; 5:28; 1 Corinthians 15:50-58). The apostle Paul expresses it this way, "For to me, to live is Christ and to die is gain" (Philippians 2:21). In other words, if I continue living in the physical body, I live for Christ, and if I die, I go to heaven. This is a twice win relationship. Believers in Jesus Christ are winners both in life and in death. In fact, death is not really death, it is a mode of transition to heaven. "For to be absent from the body is to be present with the Lord" (2 Corinthians 5:1-9).

Furthermore, the Word of God informs us, "As in Adam all die, even so in Christ shall all be made alive. But each in turn: Christ, the firstfruits; then when he come, those who belong to him (1Corinthians 15: 22-23). Jesus conquers death for us and opens Paradise for all. But all will not go to Paradise or heaven because not all have a relationship with Jesus Christ. The unregistered will perish (John 3:16).

Steps to Registration

Step #1: *You must repent of your sins or perish* (Acts 2:37-38). God sees you and me as sinners under the wrath of God, as rebels against divine law. Unless we change, we are on our way to eternal condemnation (John 3:16-19). Most of us are not murderers, robbers, liars, immoral or fraudsters; we are good people by this world's standard. That will get us in big trouble, because we tend to think we have nothing to repent of.

But we need to see ourselves as God sees us, sinners, condemned, in need of a Savior, and we cannot save ourselves. He calls upon us to accept His help and repent. Repentance is a change of mind, attitude, lifestyle, and direction. It is godly sorrow for the wrongful life we have lived, a turnaround from the direction we are going to the way God offers us.

Repentance is required! It was required under the Old Testament (OT) Isaiah 1:2-20). And now it is required under the New Testament (NT). John the Baptist was the last of the OT prophets and the forerunner of the ministry of Jesus Christ. He prepared Israel for the coming of the Messiah, and he preached repentance (Matthew 3:1-12; Mark 1: 4-5).

Jesus started His ministry preaching repentance (Matthew 3:12-17). He came to save His people from their sins (Matthew 1:21). Jesus commanded His disciples to preach repentance in His name beginning at Jerusalem (Luke 24: 45-49). The apostles started their ministry preaching repentance (Acts 2:27-38).

Again, repentance means change; with the help of God's grace, you must give up the old lifestyle. The liar gives up lying, the thief gives up stealing, the sexually immoral gives up that life as you are born a new into the kingdom of God (John 3:5).

Step #2: *You must call on Jesus to have mercy on you*, to forgive you, to come into your heart and change your life.

Genuine repentance includes acknowledgement of your sins, confession of your sins to the Lord, asking the Lord to forgive you, and a resolve with the help of God to turn away from that lifestyle. King David after some serious sins cried out to God for mercy and forgiveness (Psalm 51:1-19). David confessed his sins to God; we are asked to do the same: acknowledge, confess, and turn away from our sins (Romans 10:9-10; 1John 1:8-10).

Step #3: Practice devotional Bible reading, and a consistent prayer life. First buy a Bible from Amazon.com or from Christianbooks.com. Preferably a study Bible, New King James (NKJ) or the New International Version (NIV) translation. Read a portion daily; this is your devotional reading. Start reading in the Gospel of John in the New Testament. Set aside a few hours two or three times a week that you can study more extensively. Study one book of the Bible at a time.

Talk to the Lord every chance you get, especially before going to bed at night, and first thing when you get up in the morning. A consistent prayer life is necessary.

Step #4: Begin to fellowship with other Christians by attending regularly a Bible believing church. That is a church where they preach and live the Bible. True followers of Christ are loving people, not gossipers, not haters. After a short period of attending, you should feel accepted and loved.

But remember, there are no perfect people or churches. Satan also attend church; it is where he recruits. So, you will encounter him more frequently at church. Be alert always! At times Satan appears like an angel of light. Do not let him trip you up!

Step #5: Ask the pastor or a deacon to have you prepared for water baptism by immersion, not sprinkling. When you are baptized by immersion, the whole body goes under the water and up out of the water as Jesus did (Matthew 3:13-17, 28:19-20).

Accept sprinkling only if there is a severe water shortage in the region, and access to clean river or sea water is not available or appropriate for baptism. A well-organized church will have new members class that you attend before or after baptism.

Step #6: Get involved in the life of the fellowship or church. Attend regularly and give regularly (Acts 2:42-47; Hebrews 10:25). A good practice is tithes and offering; it is the method God uses to support the work of His kingdom on earth. Tithes is giving a tenth of what God blesses you with (Malachi 3:8-11). Offering is any amount you feel to give (2 Corinthians 9:6-15).

But do not give out of guilt, shame, or coercion, as some churches are in the habit of doing. Let no one pressure you in this regard or put you under obligation.

Step #7: Practice witnessing. Witnessing is sharing Jesus and His gospel to others, so that they too can become His disciples, and join the community of believers (Matthew 28:18-20). One easy way to do this is to share your faith experience with family, friends, neighbors, and even enemies (Acts 1:8).

Jesus won His disciples one by one; as one found Jesus, he called another (John 1:29-51). Jesus used the one-to-one method frequently and effectively. He won the woman at the well using the one-to-one method; we call it personal evangelism (John 4). Jesus also preached and teach large crowds, but the one-to-one method is immensely powerful. The story of Zacchaeus is another good example of one-to-one witnessing (Luke 19:1-10).

By sharing your faith and by using you your talents and gifts in the life of the church to the glory of God, you can make a significant difference in the kingdom of God. However, do not over-extend yourself; you cannot be in everything. A river that spreads itself too wide becomes a stagnant swamp. But if you harness that water, you could light a city.

Step #8: *Guard against distractions.* Remember, Satan goes to church too. In fact, church is a fertile recruiting ground for Satan, Guard against people who entice you to sin, people who are argumentative and contentious, they are always causing conflicts. Some people go to the building with the name church on it, but they are not followers of Christ, and they do not know.

Step #9: Self-evaluation. The best way to do this is to set goals for your spiritual growth and development and self-check every three months how you are doing. Are you growing in the Lord? Are you being spiritually fed at this church?

You may want to select another believer as your accountable spiritual partner to keep you on the straight and narrow path. Meet every now and then for honest feedback. Of course, the person you select must be a serious, well grounded, mature, Holy Spirit filled believer. These nine steps will guide you through the registration process and more.

Online Registration Screening

Some people may want to begin with Online Registration Screening (ORS) then the preceding nine **Offline** steps.

First, ORS provides answers to lifestyle issues that are not in keeping with the biblical text and therefore cannot be authentic in heavenly registration, if embraced as continuing practice.

Repentance calls for the abandonment of all unbiblical and immoral lifestyles. An adulterer, a thief, a liar, a fornicator, a homosexual or any other, cannot be a child of heaven and actively practicing that lifestyle. We are not saved in our sins; we are saved from our sins (Matthew 1:21). God does not give an exception to any sin. There is no sin that the grace of God is not sufficient to give you the victory over.

Secondly, ORS provides a supportive community for all registrants. Everyone, therefore, is invited to participate in ORS (see **Appendix A** at the back of this book for details).

Registration Process in Heaven

Registration has two faces, one in heaven, the other on earth. An authentic registration is when the practice of earth meets the requirements of heaven. One must be the mirror image of the other. The Word of God contains the requirement of heaven. It does not bend to accommodate the registrant; the registrants must bend to comply. The Word of God is not suggestions to be ignored or negotiate; it is an executive order to comply with.

Therefore, if a local church on earth have members who have not repented of their sins, received God's forgiveness through a born-again experience, those members are not registered in the Lamb's Book of Life in heaven. They have ignored what heaven requires. As a result, they are traveling with a false sense of security. Some sinful habits require fasting and prayer to break.

What kind of record-keeping system heaven has? Why is it necessary, and how does the process work? I will try to answer these three questions in this section without being carried away with too much speculation on why.

The Bible does not directly answer the why question. But we can deduce the why answer from what an instrument is used for. You may not know why a neighbor has a particular instrument in his backyard until you see him at work using it; the use explains the why or purpose.

The kingdom of God keeps records of all people who have lived and currently living upon earth, including the people of God who are citizens of heaven. God has personal knowledge on each person; He knows our motives and intensions. He knows us intimately, better than we know ourselves (Psalms 139:1-13).

Despite His comprehensive knowledge of us and all that transpire in His creation, God uses the assistance of millions of angels of various ranks and power in the administration of His kingdom. There are ordinary angels, archangels, seraphim, and cherubim, principalities, and powers, among others (Isaiah 6:1-3;1 Thessalonians 4:16-18; Revelation 4-6).

Angels are ministering spirits to believers (Hebrews 1:13-14). With all that—God has chosen to keep detail records on humans. A caring king and father would be knowledgeable about his citizens and his children. God is both King and Father.

The Word of God identifies heaven's recording keeping system as two set of books: the Lamb's Book of Life and the Books of Wrath. The former keeps information on the righteous who are the people of God. The latter records the deeds of unbelievers or unrighteous (for detail, see my book, The Book of Life & The Books of Wrath, second edition).[1]

The time of history the Bible was written, books were in scroll format. When communicating to humans, God normally use that which is familiar to us. If the Bible were given to us in the 21st century, perhaps the record-keeping system in heaven would be shown as a supercomputer, because we are familiar with that kind of record keeping system.

When are names registered to the Lambs book of life? There are two possible answers to this question. (1) Since the Bible says we were chosen from the foundation of the world, from God's perspective we are registered from that time (Ephesians 1: 4-6). (2) But from human perspective, we are registered at the point in time we are born again into the kingdom of God and adopted into the His family (John 3:5; Romans 8:14-17).

The Bible informs us that there is rejoicing in heaven among the angels when someone repents or is newly born into the kingdom of God (Luke 15:3-10). This could be nothing less than a birthday celebration. In addition to celebration, birth is always accompanied by some official documentation, such as a birth certificate. And it makes sense that the angels get involved with us from the very beginning of our spiritual life, because they are given the assignment of ministering to us who are the heirs of salvation (Hebrews1:14).

For what is the information in the book of life used? The book of life contains the service record of believers. By believers, I mean those who are born again into the kingdom of God and are adopted into the family of God (John 3:5; Romans 8:4-17, 23). While they do not work to acquire salvation, they are expected to serve Christ faithfully after salvation is received, and they will be rewarded for that service rendered out of love for the Lord.

Their information is used to reward them at or after the *Believers Judgment.* First Corinthians 3:8-15 is one passage among many that addresses this issue of reward in heaven. Second Corinthians 5:10 is one scripture passage that refers to the Believers' Judgment, among others.

Believers will be judged in heaven but not for their sins, so they will not be condemned or thrown out of heaven for any reason. If they are in heaven they are among the chosen. The apostle Paul reminds us that "there is no condemnation to those who are in Christ Jesus" (Romans 8:1).

God does not keep a sin record on believers, because their sins are atoned for in the work of Jesus Christ on the cross, forgiven, and forgotten (Jeremiah 31:31-34; Hebrews10:17). But believers will be judged for their works, works done in the name of the Lord. We are required to be faithful and serve Christ out of Love. That is the kind of service that He will reward.

A great deal of work done using the name of the Lord is for selfish reasons; it is not Jesus the workers were honoring or love. They love self or the unrighteous mammon, money! They say,

Lord, Lord, but their hearts are far from the Lord. Such people will receive no reward when their service records are reviewed at the Believers' Judgment. Jesus in Matthew 6 repeatedly warn against this very thing, loss rewards, not loss heaven.

For details and a deeper understanding of what will transpire at the believers' judgment, see Volume 2 in the series, "Related Events to the Second Coming of the Christ" by this author. The title is, *The Believes' Judgment and Rewards* for details.[2]

Let me emphasize, only registrants of the Lamb's book of life will enter heaven (Hebrews 12:22-23). Revelation 20:15 gives us this intelligence report, "Anyone whose name was not found written in the book of life was thrown into the lake of fire." It is for this reason and more that unbelievers are urgently invited to register now by repenting of their sins and establishing a saving relationship with Jesus Christ.

At the same time believers are warned to examine carefully how they serve Jesus, because their whole life of service can go up in flames, and they receive no reward in heaven for it.

Summation

In this chapter we cover the fact that registration to the Lamb's Book of Life in heaven is both a human and divine process. The human side is what you the registrant must do to comply with the registration requirements of Scripture. You must repent of your sins and establish a relationship with Jesus Christ.

Nine steps are given to complete the process. But the relationship with Jesus Christ is established by step #4. Step 5 is baptism in water; you are baptized because you have already received Jesus as your Savior and Lord.

The divine side of registration is deep and complex, but the simple side is that we are sanctified (made clean), we are justified (made righteous), and there is a celebration that takes place in heaven among the angels, and our names are entered in the book of life.

Throughout your life-long Christian journey, you have certain responsibilities such as obeying the word of God, living a clean life, staying in fellowship, and give your time in loving, faithful service to Christ.

CHAPTER 6

THE DESTINY OF THE UNREGISTERED

The book of life is not the only record-keeping system in heaven, as you have already observed. There are other books or scrolls. I label these *"The Books of Wrath"* (see Revelation 5-6 and chapter 20:12).

Whose records are kept in the Books of Wrath, when were these names entered, and for what is the information used? We will try to answer these questions briefly in this chapter. For a more comprehensive discussion, see the second edition of my book, *The Book of Life and The Books of Wrath.*[1]

When people are born into this world, they are automatically enrolled in the books of wrath. This is not complicated because we were conceived in sin, shaped in iniquity, and born in sin (Psalm 51:5; Romans 5:12). So, we were born in the state of sin even though we did not yet commit sin as an act. Therefore, the appropriate book of enrollment is the books of wrath. In fact, we are recorded in heaven before we were born (Psalm 139:13-16).

We come into this world in a state of sin and enrolled in the books of wrath. For this reason, we need a new birth experience to be registered into the Lamb's book of life in kingdom of God as Jesus informs us (John 3:5, 16). At the time of our new birth experience, we cross over from death to life (Ephesian 2:1-2).

But for those who have not cross-over, their names remain in the books of wrath, and if they remain in that state of sin until physical death comes to them without being born again, they inherit eternal death. Eternal life is for the born-again ones.

Now there are certain years of life that a child is innocent and is not responsible. The years of accountability differ with each child. The justice of God takes all that into consideration. Even human courts treat children differently. So, there is no need to be concerned about the death of infants and minors who have not reached the age of accountability; God has them covered.

When a person repents of his or her sins and is born again into the kingdom of God, that person is moved from the books of wrath to the book of life. Again, the Bible says, "we cross over from death to life" (John 5:24). A transfer of names take place in heaven from the *Books of Wrath* to the *Book of Life*.

But if a person does not repent but continues to reject Jesus Christ and the salvation He offers, that person will remain in the books of wrath and becomes a candidate for the second death, also called eternal death (Revelation 20:14). After physical death, that person will be resurrected, judged for his or her sins at the final judgment and thrown into the eternal lake of burning sulfur, also known as hell (John 5:28; Revelation 20:6, 11-15).[2]

The final judgment for unbelievers is called the *white throne* judgment; it is evidence based (Revelation 20:11-12). Courts of law in our society render decisions based upon five levels of evidence: 1) "reasonable suspicion," 2) "probable cause," 3) "preponderance of the evidence," 4) "clear and convincing evidence," and 5) "evidence beyond a reasonable doubt."[3]

Only one of these categories is needed for rendering the decision at the *white throne judgment*, and it is the highest category, evidence beyond a reasonable doubt. Why? First, God is eyewitness to all that transpire in His creation; nothing is hid from His eyes. "All things are opened and naked before the eyes of Him with whom we have to do" (Hebrews 4:13 KJV).

God also sees the motive behind each action, so He knows why we do what we do. The prophet Samuel declares, "Man sees the outward appearance, but God sees the heart" (1Samuel 16:7). Motives are particularly important in a court of law in the determination of guilt or innocence. God weighs our motives.

Second, despite His omniscience, God deploys millions of angels in His administration that document what transpires in His kingdom. In human courts video and DNA are compelling evidence used to establish guilt or innocence. God is the primary inventor of these methods; He revealed these methods of knowledge to humans; humans claim originality. But God is the source of all knowledge, He created the tree of knowledge and planted it within the reach of humans (Genesis 2: 8-9).

Despite the varied and voluminous evidence available to God at the judgment, one should not entertain the notion that human cases will be debated at the judgment. There will be no debate; the evidence will be so overwhelming that your own mouth will pronounce yourself guilty and justly deserving of the penalty accorded. Each person will see his or her life unfolded in vivid color with evidence beyond reasonable doubt.

This is the court of supreme and final justice. There is no appellate division in God's court of justice; the rendering is final and cannot be overruled.

If believers are at this judgment, they are there as assistants to the judge, not as the ones to be judged. The apostle Paul rebuked the church at Corinth for carrying their disputes before the heathen court for settlement instead of settling their differences among themselves. He said, "Do you not know that that the Lord's people will judge the world? And if you are to judge the world, are you not competent to judge trivial cases? Do you not know that we will judge angels? How much the things of this life" (1 Corinthians 6:1-4).

Based on the evidence, all rebels against His Majesty's government and authority will have their sentence of eternal death carried out as recorded in the open books of wrath (Revelation 20:11-15). There will be weeping and gnashing of teeth, but the justice of the court will prevail.

Unbelievers have been under the unreleased wrath of God all their lives but most of them do not know it (John 3:18-21). Why don't they know it? During the time of their lives, they enjoy the common grace goodness and blessing of the Lord, with the hope that His goodness would lead them to repentance (Romans 2:4). For some, the goodness of God has moved them to repentance. But for others, it magnifies and multiplies their wickedness because they credit their success and prosperity to their own genius rather than to the goodness of God.

Some people who persist in their wickedness eventually have the wrath of God released upon them during their lifetime.

Human wickedness can become so deep and widespread that God give them up (Romans 1:18-32). Sometimes God surgically remove the wicked from among humankind as was the case of Sodom and Gomorrah (Genesis 19:1-29).

Nobody goes to hell ignorantly or blindly because God has revealed Himself in creation, human history, and in His Son Jesus Christ (Psalm 19:1-6; Hebrews 1:1-4). Humans know that the path they have chosen leads to eternal life or eternal destruction (Matthew 7:13-14; John 3:16). God has clearly revealed Himself, so they are without excuse (Romans 1:20).

Like a car about to use the wrong off-ramp exit to enter a major highway—it first marks, "Do Not Enter, Wrong Way!" Then every now and then the sign, "Wrong Way" appears. Only a reckless person who does not care for his life or the lives of others would keep going. Eventually disaster will come. The unbeliever is not ignorant of the road he or she is travelling on because there are numerous warnings posted.

God is mighty, patient, and compassionate toward humans; He gives us a long time to repent and turn from our wicked ways. He helps us to change, if we genuinely want to change. But He is not going to hogtie us and force us into heaven against our will. We are free moral agents and God respects that.

The Destiny of Unregistered People

Being born again into the kingdom of God is a human and divine partnership (John 3:5, 16). God does the heavy lifting by provide the sacrifice, His Word as roadmap, and the assistance of the blessed Holy Spirit. He also provides a community of believers called the Church, to encourage and nurture us on our pilgrimage. We are called upon to believe, repent of our sins, and accept the sacrifice, God's forgiveness, enjoin ourselves to a fellowship of people of like faith, and live by the Word oof God.

If we refuse to accept and follow this provision of God in Jesus Christ, we are saying to God, we will charter our own way and be responsible for the consequences. Like Adam and Eve standing before the tree of death from which they were forbidden to eat, we know the consequence that will befall us.

With eyes wide open Adam and Eve ate and died because they believe the serpent's lie over God's truth. If with eyes wide opened or closed we reject God's provision of salvation in Jesus Christ, we are eternally lost, and we will be sentenced at the Final Judgment to the eternal lake of burning sulfur as our final destination. In essence, we send ourselves there by our freedom of choice. God respects our freedom of choice. But who are the unregistered?

Who are the Unregistered?

We have stated repeatedly throughout this book who the unregistered are. We called them unbelievers, those who are not born again, the unconverted, those who reject Jesus Christ and His salvation. At the risk of being redundant, we come to the question again by listing them by category.

First, the unregistered are all the people who reject Jesus Christ and His plan of salvation. This is a universal category because all unregistered people reject Jesus Christ. Their names are not in the Lamb's book of life in heaven because they are not born-again; they will perish (John 3:5,16).

We can protest this premise; we can buck and rant that it is not fair until hell itself freezes over, but all that will not change the Word of God. We may want to setup a system more favorable to us, but that too will be an exercise in futility. God determines who and how we get into His heaven. We take it or leave it.

Second, there are morally good people by this world's standard, but their self-righteousness is not good enough to qualify them for the *Book of Life*. All religion have some form of goodness or righteousness, but not what God accepts. The practice of those religions may make you a good citizen of earth, but certainly not of heaven.

Third, there are religious people who are certain that their religion secures them a place in heaven. They think that their religion is the right one and they are superior to other people. They are ritualistic, devoted, and often so holy they cannot mingle with other humans. Frankly, they come in all stripes.

Some of them are baptized in water, members of churches, preachers of various ranks, rabbi, theology professors, miracle workers. They profess to work for Jesus, but He does not know them. He does not have a saving relationship with them, so their names are not in the Lamb's book of life (Matthew 7:21-23).

They may have a good story. They may have magical powers to command people to rise from their wheelchairs and disabled people to throw away their crutches and run and leap on stage before a television audience. But if they are not born-again with an authentic relationship with Jesus Christ, they are not registered in the Lamb's Book of Life. Jesus will say to them, "Depart from me you workers of iniquity, I does not know you."

In the time of Jesus, first century AD, these were Scribes, Pharisees, and Sadducees. Jesus called them hypocrites, blind guides. They eventually conspired and had Him crucified.

Fourth, there are people who do not claim to be morally good or religious and they have nothing to do with Jesus. These, like the others, are considered lost.

Revelation 20:12 clearly states that all the people whose names are not found written in the book of life are thrown into the lake of fire. When we read this, we begin stuttering with monosyllabic words like but, but, if, if, that is not fair. We do not get to decide what is fair from what is not. Let God be God. We are creatures, mere mortals. If you want to get into heaven, register by using the guidelines the Word of God provides.

CHAPTER 7

BENEFITS OF BEING REGISTRED

W hat benefits will registrants to the Lamb's Book of Life in heaven receive? The benefits are numerous; they cannot be fully documented. But that is not the only reason. Most of the benefits are classified, others are partly revealed.

Therefore, we can only speak briefly on what is already revealed in the Word of God, and even those, details are not given. The Bible informs us that "eye has not seen, and ear has not heard, nor has it entered into the heart of man, the things God has prepared for them that love him" (1Corinthians 2:9).

The context to preceding quote tells us that some things are revealed to God's people by the Holy Spirit, but the secret things belong to God. He reveals them to humans on a need-to-know basis, not so much when humans need to know, but when God thinks they need to know. There have been mysteries, hidden knowledge, kept in God for ages not revealed to humans or angels until the fulness of time (1 Corinthians 2:7-8).

There are things that were kept secret from prophets, priests, and kings in the Old Testament (OT) that are now revealed in the Church age. But there are still classified things hidden in God, not yet revealed. One of them is the day God will call for His people. Jesus instructed His people to watch for in such an hour when they least expect, the Son of Man will come (Matthew 24:36-44). This warning is repeated throughout the NT.

Humans always want to know what is in it for them before they commit to any venture; that is the way we are wired, and that is a good thing. It signals that we value our time, and we want to be compensated for it. And that is the way God wants it because He is the one who invented the work ethic and the work week. God gave man his first job, and a family to support (Genesis 2:1-25). Genesis opens with God Himself at work.

When we register for heaven, we are making a lifetime commitment to work for the kingdom of God and abide by the rules and culture of His kingdom. We are not just registering to save our skin from the fires of hell. If that is what you think, you got it wrong! Upon registering, you become part of the work force of the kingdom of God on earth. And the benefits are great! You could not have a better boss or work for a better enterprise. But be careful how you serve; we are not redeemed to serve ourselves. We are saved to serve Christ faithfully out of love.

What is in it for Us?

Before you commit yourself, it is wise to ask, what is in it for me? Jesus called His first disciples away from their occupation of fishing. These men had families to feed; Peter had a wife and perhaps children (Matthew 4:18-22). Matthew worked for the government as a tax collector. This was a lucrative job to give up to follow an itinerant preacher from Nazareth.

But to these men, Jesus was more than an ordinary preacher from a peasant community. They believed He was the long-awaited Messiah of Israel; that He was the one to restore the nation to its golden years of Kings David and Solomon, and they would be top executives in His kingdom. For them that would be status, prestige, and wealth. But all Jesus said to them was, "Come, follow me and I will make you fishers of men" (Matthew 4:18-22). He did not promise them worldly power, prestige, and wealth. It was their active imagination that filled in the blanks. Their understanding of the Messiah was flawed.

At first, they had no idea what Jesus' true mission was all about. And it was not a mission He could explain to them in one sitting. Yes, Jesus came to establish a kingdom but not the one His disciples had in mind. They were looking for a Him to throw off the oppressive Roman yoke and restore the Jewish State.

But Jesus had no intention of restoring the Jewish State at that time. He came to establish a spiritual kingdom, the rule of God in the hearts of humankind. He referred to it as the kingdom of heaven or the kingdom of God; He explains it in His parables and other teaching stories. This was a difficult concept for the disciples to grasp, and they did not fully get it up to the time of His ascension (Acts 1:6-11). It was most difficult for them to see a kingdom in their interest that was not the Jewish State.

But whether a spiritual kingdom or the Jewish State, Jesus did not call and commission them to work in His kingdom for free. Jesus' encounter with the rich, young ruler sheds light upon the disciples' understanding of Jesus' mission and the question of compensation (Matthew 19:16-29).

The rich young ruler, as he is commonly called, asked what he should do to inherit eternal life. Jesus told him to keep the Law of God. But the young man responded that from his youth he had kept the Law perfectly. This response suggests that despite keeping the Law of Moses flawlessly he had an aching, spiritual void his religious practices did not satisfy. The Law did not give him the eternal life he was now seeking from Jesus.

Jesus then made a greater demand upon the young man. He said, "If you want to be perfect, go sell your possessions and give to the poor, and you will have treasure in heaven. Then come follow me" (verse 21). That was too much to ask.

The young man could not part with his wealth to follow Jesus or give it up for the greater wealth of eternal life, so he left sorrowful. He weighed his riches against the gift of eternal life and chose his earthly wealth instead. The irony is, he chose what he could not keep over what he could not lose, had he chosen it. All earthly riches are temporary; treasures stored in heaven are lasting (Matthew 6:19-24).

The disciples were astounded, not so much of the young man walking away, but that Jesus made such unreasonable demand on him, wanting him to part with his wealth to follow Him. They were even most shocked, flabbergasted at what Jesus said about rich people after the young man left.

He said, "Truly I tell you; it is hard for someone who is rich to enter the kingdom of heaven." He did not stop there, He went on to say, Again, I tell you, it is easier for a camel to go through the eye of a needle than for someone who is rich to enter the kingdom of God" (Matthew 19: 23-24).

This information cause jaw-dropping astonishment for the disciples because they thought earthly wealth was a sign of God's approval and blessing. Now they are hearing that it is almost incompatible with the kingdom of God. Their protest was as if saying, "We did not sign up for a poverty cult!"

Peter blurted out, "We have forsaken all to follow you, what is in it for us?" (verse 27). Wow! Things got really tense upon this astonishing revelation on what Jesus' mission and the kingdom of God are all about. It is not about getting rich!

Peter's question, posed on behalf of all the disciples, was a question of compensation that any rational human being would have asked. What is in it for us? He was saying, we did not sign up for this! We had occupations, we had income producing businesses, and we have forsaken all to follow you, and now this.

This was a tense moment fraught with emotions, as they stared at the sobering reality about the kingdom of God. Jesus needed to urgently calm things down with a more satisfactory theology of material possession and wealth. He said to them:

> Truly I tell you, at the renewal of aa things, when the Son of Man sits on his glorious throne, you who have followed me will also sit on twelve thrones judging the twelve tribes of Israel.

> And everyone who has left houses or brothers or sisters or father or mother or wife or children or fields for my sake will receive a hundred times as much and will inherit eternal life. But many who are first will be last, and many who are last will be first. (Matthew 19: 28-30)

The preceding explanation was both long term and short term for His immediate disciples; it has implications for the wider Church as well. It addresses the eternal life aspect of the kingdom as well as the short-term compensation issue for the here and now. The disciples did not abandon Jesus at this time to return to their former occupations or anytime thereafter. But it did not completely clear up the kingdom of heaven and its relationship with the restoration of the Jewish State.

They continued to ask Jesus about the time of that restoration to the day of His ascension (Acts 1:6-11). Certain mysteries about the spiritual kingdom, including the Church and the Jewish State were further revealed to the great apostles Paul and John in the apocalypse.

The apostles preached the gospel with a better understanding of the kingdom of heaven, and they all had their material needs well provided for. Many who follow Jesus today are millionaires many times over. They eat and dress well, they live in luxurious mansions and travel the world in private jets. But money and the abundance of things possessed, are not the most important benefits or what the kingdom of God is truly about.

We came into this world naked and void of lugged and we will not take anything with us when we depart. So, what are the true and more lasting benefits when you are registered in the Lamb's book of life? Let us briefly unpack from the Word of God few of the things that are revealed.

The Benefits of Registration

As stated earlier, the benefits are too numerous for anyone book or set of encyclopedias to document. Furthermore, most benefits are classified or partly revealed. In this section, therefore, I will briefly discuss a few of the benefits revealed in the Scriptures.

First, the benefit of forgiveness of sin. This is the first gift from God experienced after repentance. It is a gateway gift that stays with us. God requires repentance on our part and the gift of forgiveness on His part. In the acts of repentance, we see ourselves as a lost sinner who offends God and stands under His wrath. We are penitent and sorrowful for what we have done, and that moves us to cry out to God for mercy and forgiveness as king David did in Psalm 51, and as the apostle Paul instructed us in Romans 10:9-10.

Let me emphasize, forgiveness is a gift we receive from God when we genuinely repent of our sins. It is a gift made possible because of the sacrifice of Jesus Christ on the cross. It is a very costly gift; it cost God the life of His Son (John 3:14-16). God remits our sins and gives us a clean slate. From now on we walk in forgiveness. The heavy burden of guilt and condemnation are removed from our shoulders, and we now walk in freedom (Matthew 11:28-30; Galatians 5:1).

Not only that—but once forgiven, we are also required to offer the gift of forgiveness to others when they offend us and later cry out to us for mercy. This is the way we secure future and continued forgiveness from God (Matthew 6:12-14). So, forgiveness is not a one-time act of God, nor should it be on our part. Peter asked Jesus, "Lord, how many times shall I forgive my brother or sister who sins against me? Up to seven times?" Jesus replied, "I tell you, not seven times, but seventy times seven (Matthew 18:21-22). In other words, always forgive.

Forgiveness must become part of our worship life, not only asking for it when we confess in our prayers and give it in our Christian interactions but give thanks to God always for such a gift. The Psalm 103 list forgiveness as a benefit received from the Lord and for which we must bless Him at all times. The people who are registered in the Lamb's book of life in heaven are those who are forgiven, their sin question is settled.

***Second, the benefit of eternal life* (John 3:14-16).** The magnitude of this gift is partly revealed and partly classified; it is also foundational to all the other gifts. Eternal life is resident in the person of Jesus Christ; it is not gifted to humans outside of a salvation relationship with Jesus (Romans 6:23). That relationship must be established before you die physically, or the opportunity to possess it is forever lost.

Eternal life is more than longevity of life; it is a quality of life not yet fully revealed, but it will be perfect and lived in a perfect environment. For that reason, the old order of thing will be done away with: Satan, sin, suffering, disease, death, and the like. A new heaven and earth will be brought into play to live the quality of life that is eternal. The minds of humans cannot fully grasp that now. You can see why I said, it is partly classified.

Eternal life guarantees a life beyond death; it includes being resurrected from the dead and an existence that cannot die again (John 5:28; 1Thessalonians 4:16-18). Death was a result of sin; both are enemies that will be destroyed. God will have no further use for them in His creation (1Corinthian 15:50-58; Revelation 20:11-15). Upon your registration in the book of life, you are gifted and guaranteed eternal life, so even if you die physically, you will rise again to die no more (John 5:28).

Of those who died or will die, Jesus is the first to rise; He alone is in the firstfruits category from among the dead. Those of us who believe in Him will be in the general resurrection harvest at His coming (1Corinthians 15:50-56). We will rise not just to meet Him but to reign with Him. For details, see my book, *RESURRECTION OF HUMANS, Guaranteed Life after Life*.

Third, we are given citizenship in the Kingdom of God and sonship in His family ((Romans 8:14-17; Philippians 3:20). We are born again into the Kingdom of God, and that gives us the right of citizenship (John 3:5). Our adoption into the family of God gives us the right of sonship. We are made heirs and co-heirs with Jesus Christ who is the only begotten Son of God. The benefits of registration keep getting better.

Fourth, we are given access to God eternally. The moment we are brought into relationship with Jesus Christ, we are given access to God the Father. All this is based upon the sacrifice of Jesus Christ our Lord (Romans 5:1-5). This access is possible because the wall of partition between God and His people was demolished by the work of Jesus Christ on the cross. The rending of the curtain that separated the holy from the most holy place in the temple took place while Jesus was on the cross (Matthew 27: 50-56). The tearing of the curtain is symbolic; it signals to us that the barrier between God and His people is forever removed (Ephesians 2: 13-22).

Access to God is *immediate*. This means that the moment you repent of your sins, receive forgiveness, and a relationship with the Lord is established, you are not only registered in heaven, but you also have intimate access to God the Father (Matthew 6: 9-13). Hebrews 4:16 (KJV) tells us, "Let us therefore come boldly to the throne of grace that we may obtain mercy and find grace to help in our time of need."

How do we get into God's presence? It is through acts of worship but let us break it down in three:

1) In a general way, we the children of God are always in His presence. We can call on Him anywhere, anytime. We cannot get away from His care (Psalm 139:7-12).

2) When we assemble in corporate worship, we enter God's presence in a unique way of reverence and confidence, not terrified as the ancient Israelites at the foothills of Sinai. We join with "an innumerable company of angels" of varying ranks and the saints above who are already made perfect in Jesus Christ (Hebrews 12:18-24; Psalm 95:1-7). The Apostle's Creed refers to the "communion of saints," which some believe points to as the saints above who join us in worship as part of the "cloud of witness" referenced in Hebrews 12:1 (KJV).

3) When we worship privately, we also enter into the presence of the Lord. I am speaking of our individual, devotional life which includes our prayer time (Matthew 6:5-13; Hebrews 4:16).

Our access to God is not only immediate; *it is also eternal* which means, there will be no end to it. It is eternal and progressive in the sense that we keep getting closer to God as more of Him is revealed to us. How? The time is coming when God will relocate to dwell with us and we with Him and we will see Him face to face (Revelation 21:1-4).

Fifth, the people of God will be given an eternal inheritance in the kingdom of God, that is reserved for each of us heaven (1Peter1:3-5). It is gifted to all those who are born again into the kingdom God and adopted into the family of God.

As children of God, we are made co-heirs with Jesus Christ and share in what the Fathers own, which is everything. Psalm 24:1-2 reminds us that the earth and everything in it belongs to

God. And Romans (8:14-17) speaks to our inheritance based on family relationship. Reference of the believers' inheritance was made earlier in this volume, so no more needs to be said here.

A distinction was also made between the believers' reward and the believers inheritance. Reward is earned but inheritance is gifted and based upon family relationship. A believer can lose his or her reward but not the inheritance. For more on this, I refer you to two of my other publications: *The Believers' Judgment and Rewards*, and *The Book of Life and the Books of Wrath*.

Sixth, the people of God will occupy the new creation. The new creation includes: the new heaven, the new earth, and the New Jerusalem, which is the Universal capital. God's people will have unlimited access (Revelation 21:1-5). For more details on this, see my book, *The New World Order.*

Seventh, the people of God who are registered in heaven have entered God's special blessings and live under it now here on earth. God provides for our material and spiritual needs. Love, joy, peace, patience, self-control, faith, and goodness are some of the graces produced in us by the blessed Holy Spirit (Galatians 5: 22-23). We see it as our Christian duties to be peacemakers, peacekeepers, and love our neighbors, even our enemies (Matthew 5:9, 43-48). We can do these things because they are already cultivated in us by the help of the Holy Spirit.

This does not mean we are free from all the difficulties of life. God became man in the person of Jesus Christ and He was not saved from life difficulties. But he had the power to overcome them and lived His best life, set the best examples, helped more people to live meaningful lives.

Registering for heaven does not mean you will suddenly get rich, famous, and without struggles in your earthly life. You might be one of the few, but I would not count on it. But I can guarantee that God will empower you to live a great life here and help many people for His glory and have the guarantee and future hope of heaven now.

Summation

The focus of this chapter is the benefits of registration; you have gotten your name in heaven's good book. What are the benefits? Frankly, the greatest benefit is registration itself, because it guarantees you a share in all that God owns. That is everything! Registration has both long-term and short-term benefits.

Short term benefits are all the blessings we receive in our earthly life, this includes things that are not pleasant. Our pain, struggles, difficulties are in mercy given, and they are working together for our good (Romans 6:23). Some short-term blessings are referred to as common grace blessings because unregistered people also enjoy them. God sends rain upon the just and the unjust. He also cares for the animal creation (Matthew 6:25-34).

Some of the long-term benefits are listed under seven categories. These blessings are eternal; they are largely part of the believers' inheritance package reserved in heaven for them. The details of the package are still classified.

Again, the full contents and blessings of our inheritance package are secured with a salvation relationship with Jesus Christ only. This salvation relationship must be in place before physical death comes to you. If it is not, then you have lost your opportunity eternally. It is for this reason registration is most urgent. Get it done now!

APPENDIX A
Online Registration
Screening (ORS)

The purpose of Online Registration Screening (ORS) is to provide support to you and ensure that your registration is in keeping with the Word of God. You can do the ORS before, during or after the nine steps in Chapter 5 of this book. The ORS is done on our ministry website at dedwellingplace.com; when you get there, click on ORS to begin.

ORS will ask you a series of personal questions that you should answer truthfully to get the proper guidance. Do not try to fool the system because in the end, you only end up fooling yourself. The outcome you receive will tell you if you are ready for registration. **Note Well:** ORS has forward looking statements and may not be available online at the time of this publication.

If you are not ready, you need to work on the things that are shown to you to get you ready. For example, let us say you are living with your girlfriend or boyfriend without the benefit of marriage. That means you are living in sin. You need to legally get married, then return to complete your registration. If you do not decide to get married, then you must terminate the intimacy part of the relationship. You should not be living together until you get married.

Incidentally, the Word of God does not approve two people of the same sex getting married (1Corinthians 6:9).

If you have already started a relationship with Jesus Christ, baptized in water, and already the member of a church, you can still do ORS to see if you are registered correctly. ORS will tell you if you are correctly registered. If not, you will need to correct what the ORS says is wrong with your registration.

Some churches and preachers are very liberal and do not abide by the Word of God, so for your own sake examine your registration against the Word of God. Do not confuse yourself by discussing your spiritual status with every Dick, Tom, and Harry. The guidance received from ORS, or your local church should be enough. If your local church is in keeping with the Word of God ORS recommendation will only strengthen it.

ORS gives you registration basics as stated in this book. It does not tell you what local church to worship in or what denomination to affiliate yourself with.

Here are the basics of a good registration: 1) you must repent of your sins and be born again. 2) You must be baptized in water, 3) You should become member in a local fellowship that preach and live the Bible. 4) Your life must be in keeping with the Word of God. This does not mean you are going to use the Bible to beat up yourself or anyone else. Growing to maturity in Christ takes time, so be patient with yourself.

APPENDIX B

THE BOOK OF LIFE FORUM

The Book of Life Forum (BLF) is where registered people gather online to support each other. It is understood that all registrants have done the basics, even though they are from different churches or faith traditions.

The forum does not emphasize your local name church or denomination; it emphasizes your relationship with Jesus Christ. Therefore, we do tare people down as some are in the custom of doing; we builds people up because we form one body in Christ. We support, encourage, edify, and correct where necessary.

The Forum does not critique any church or faith tradition; that is not our role to sit as judge over anyone. However, if a way of life or activity clearly departs from the Word of God, we are duty bound to point that out in love, without being contentious.

However, we look at what the Word of God says about what we need to do to be registered in the Lamb's Book of Life in heaven and abide by it. We encourage each other without imposing the doctrine of any church on community members.

The Word of God presents the Church of Jesus Christ as having unity and diversity. The unity is the basics that all true church have in common: people are required to repent of their sins, be born again through a salvation experience with Jesus Christ, and they are baptized in water, and become part of the community of faith.

Though we prefer baptism by immersion, it is not always possible to have that quantity of water to baptize in some part of the world. So, we will not make that a point of contention on the Forum. In addition, we hope all registrants worship every day of the week, but there are those that gather for public to worship on a different day from Sunday. This will not be a point of contention for registrants, nor anyone will seek to impose one day over the other. There is diversity in the Body Christ, and we must embrace that diversity.

The Word of God is the standard by which we judge Christian life and practice, not what man or institution says. Yet, we respect certain traditions of the Fathers and learn from them.

Note Well: The Forum has forward looking statements and may not be available online until sometime after the publication of this book.

REFERENCES

CHAPTER 1

1. Munroe, Myles. *RELEASING YOUR POTENTIAL, Exposing the Hidden You.* Expanded Edition. PA: Destiny Image Publishers (pp.103-104), 2007.

2. Dewar, Michael W. *The New World Order.* Brooklyn, NY: Dwelling Place Publishers, 2023.

CHAPTER 2

1. The New World Order

2. Dewar Michael W. *The Millennium: A Thousand Years of Peace and Prosperity.* Brooklyn, NY: Dwelling Place Publishers, 2023.

3. _____. Series: "Related Events to the Second Coming of the Christ," Vol.7, 9,10. Amazon.com.

CHAPTER 3

1. *The Ultimate Bible Dictionary.* Revised and Expanded Edition. Nashville, TN: Holman Publishers, 2018.

2. Buttrick, George Arthur. *Chief Editor. Interpreters Dictionary of the Bible.* Vol. K-Q. Nashville, TN: Abingdon Press, 1962.

3. Sproul, R.C. *UNSEEN REALITIES, Heaven, Hell, Angels, and Demons.* Ross-shire, Scotland: Christian Focus, 2011.

4. Dewar, Michael W. *Resurrection of Humans.* Brooklyn, NY: Dwelling Place Publishers, 2023.

5. _____. *The Final Judgment.* Brooklyn, NY: Dwelling Place Publishers, 2023.

6. _____. *The Book of Life & The Books of Wrath.* Brooklyn, NY: Dwelling Place Publishers, 2023.

7. _____. *The Book of Life & The Books of Wrath.*

CHAPTER 4

1. Dewar, Michael W. *The Believers Judgment & Rewards.* Brooklyn, NY: Dwelling Place Publishers, 2023.

2. _____. The Rapture. Brooklyn, NY: Dwelling Place Publishers, 2023.

CHAPTER 5

1. Dewar, Michael W. *The Book of Life & The Books of Wrath.* Second Edition. Brooklyn, NY: Dwelling Place Publishers, 2023.

2. _____. The Believers' Judgment & Rewards. Brooklyn NY: Dwelling Place Publishers, 2023.

CHAPTER 6

1. Dewar, Michael W. *The Book of Life & The Books of Wrath.* Second Edition.

2. _____. *The Final Judgment.*

3. *Legal Standards.* https://www.nolo.com/legal-encyclopedia/legal-standards-proof.html

OTHER BOOKS BY THIS AUTHOR

Book series: "Related Events to the Second Coming of the Christ" (10-Volumes):

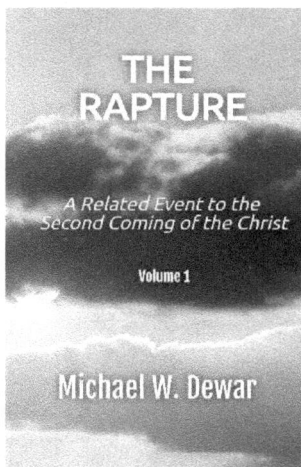

THE RAPTURE

A Related Event to the Second Coming of the Christ

Volume 1

Michael W. Dewar

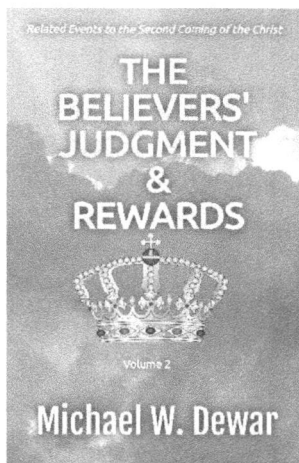

Related Events to the Second Coming of the Christ

THE BELIEVERS' JUDGMENT & REWARDS

Volume 2

Michael W. Dewar

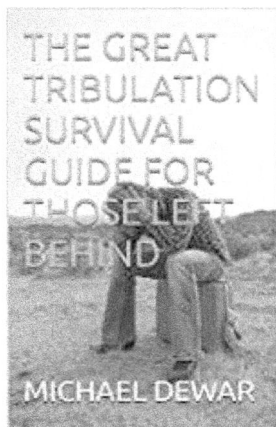

THE GREAT TRIBULATION SURVIVAL GUIDE FOR THOSE LEFT BEHIND

MICHAEL DEWAR

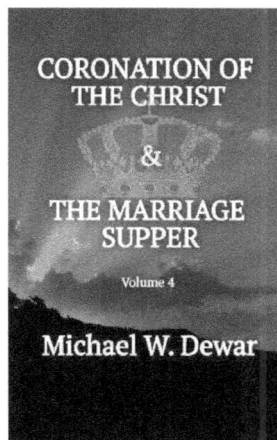

CORONATION OF THE CHRIST

&

THE MARRIAGE SUPPER

Volume 4

Michael W. Dewar

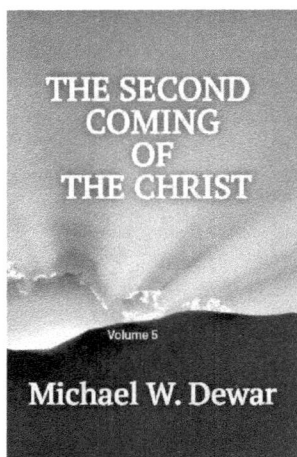

THE SECOND COMING OF THE CHRIST
Volume 5
Michael W. Dewar

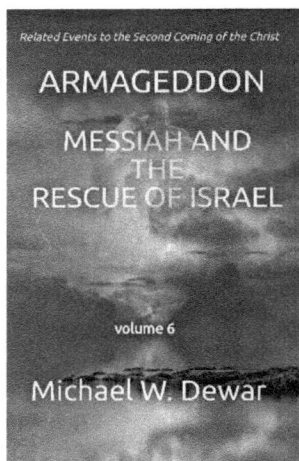

Related Events to the Second Coming of the Christ
ARMAGEDDON
MESSIAH AND THE RESCUE OF ISRAEL
volume 6
Michael W. Dewar

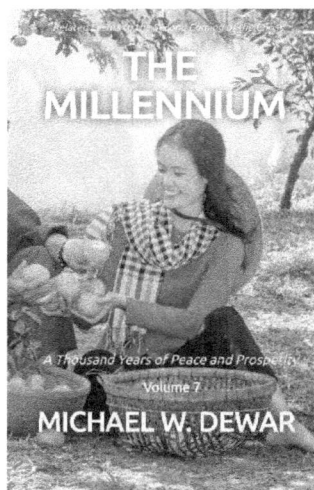

THE MILLENNIUM
A Thousand Years of Peace and Prosperity
Volume 7
MICHAEL W. DEWAR

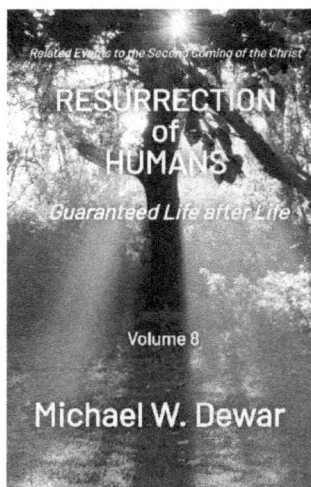

Related Events to the Second Coming of the Christ
RESURRECTION of HUMANS
Guaranteed Life after Life
Volume 8
Michael W. Dewar

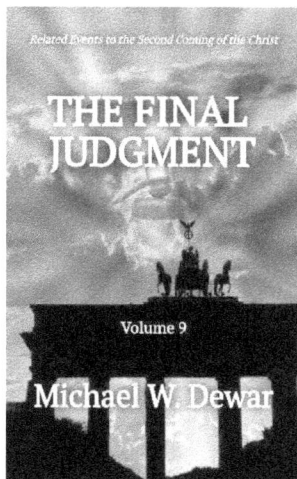

Related Events to the Second Coming of the Christ

THE FINAL JUDGMENT

Volume 9

Michael W. Dewar

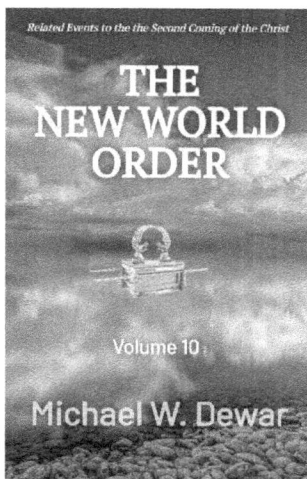

Related Events to the the Second Coming of the Christ

THE NEW WORLD ORDER

Volume 10

Michael W. Dewar

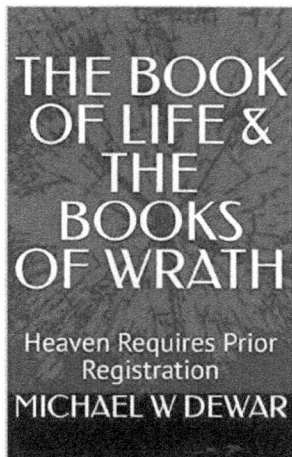

THE BOOK OF LIFE & THE BOOKS OF WRATH

Heaven Requires Prior Registration

MICHAEL W DEWAR

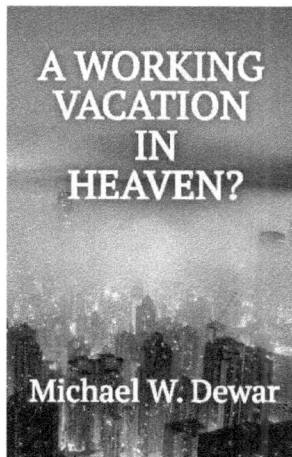

A WORKING VACATION IN HEAVEN?

Michael W. Dewar

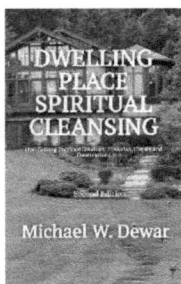

Have you had your house or dwelling spiritually cleansed? Get it done this year; this book is you guide.

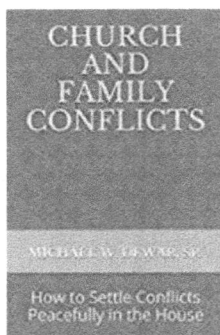

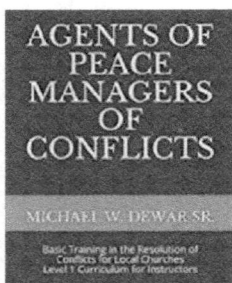

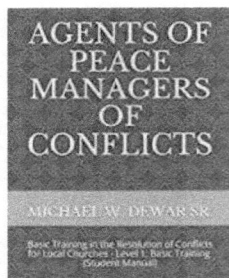

Launch a peace ministry in your church with this course of study in conflict management and resolution – Three volumes: Text book, Instructor's Manual, and Student Manual. Train agents of peace-managers of conflicts.

ABOUT THE AUTHOR

Michael W. Dewar, Sr. is a pastor, Bible teacher, and mentor in the spiritual life for more than forty years. He is also a specialist in conflict management and resolution, the author of a three-volume course on church and family conflicts, used to launch peace ministries in local churches.

He holds advanced degrees from several institutions of higher learning, including the Master of Divinity, the Master of Social Work, and an earned doctorate.

Reverend Dewar is the founder and pastor of the New York Congregational Baptist Church (NYCBC). He lives in New York with his family. He is the author of a 10-volume series on "Related Events to the Second Coming of the Christ."

Contacts:
Visit website at: DPSCleansing.com
And be sure to join the author's mailing list from there to receive updates and free give aways.

Send feedback to: CS@DPSCleansing.com

www.ingramcontent.com/pod-product-compliance
Lightning Source LLC
Chambersburg PA
CBHW022307060426
42446CB00007BA/735